AF426734

The Ultimate Salad Cookbook

Dishes, Volume 4

Olivia Bennett

Published by B&H Publishing Group, 2025.

While every precaution has been taken in the preparation of this book, the publisher assumes no responsibility for errors or omissions, or for damages resulting from the use of the information contained herein.

THE ULTIMATE SALAD COOKBOOK

First edition. February 21, 2025.

Copyright © 2025 Olivia Bennett.

ISBN: 979-8230865049

Written by Olivia Bennett.

Table of Contents

Introduction: The Art of Salad-Making..1

Chapter 1: Greens and Bases..6

Chapter 2: Dressings and Vinaigrettes.. 11

Chapter 3: Adding Texture.. 17

Chapter 4: Perfect Proteins 23

Chapter 5: Simple Side Salads 29

Chapter 6: Hearty Main Course Salads....................................... 34

Chapter 7: Healthy and Light Options 40

Chapter 8: Mediterranean-Inspired Salads 46

Chapter 9: Asian-Inspired Salads 52

Chapter 10: Latin American-Inspired Salads 58

Chapter 11: European Classics... 64

Chapter 12: Spring Salads... 69

Chapter 13: Summer Salads 75

Chapter 14: Autumn and Winter Salads..................................... 81

Chapter 15: Creative and Show-Stopping Salads....................... 87

Conclusion: The Endless Potential of Salads............................. 92

To those who believe that fresh, vibrant ingredients can turn a simple dish into something extraordinary.

To my family and friends, who have shared countless meals and memories around the table.

And to every home cook who finds joy in creating wholesome, flavorful food—may your salads always be colorful, your dressings perfectly balanced, and your creativity endless.

Here's to celebrating the art of fresh, delicious eating—one bowl at a time!

Introduction: The Art of Salad-Making

Salads, often relegated to the status of a mere side dish, have evolved into a diverse and dynamic culinary category that can be as simple or as sophisticated as desired. From their humble origins to their place in modern cuisine, salads represent a perfect union of health, flavor, and artistry. They are a celebration of fresh ingredients, a playground for creativity, and a versatile meal that can adapt to any season, culture, or occasion.

In this chapter, we'll explore why salads are more than just a side dish, dive into the fascinating history and cultural evolution of salads, and equip you with the tools, ingredients, and techniques needed to create exceptional salads that stand out in both taste and presentation.

Why Salads Are More Than Just a Side Dish

1. A Nutritional Powerhouse

Salads are often synonymous with healthy eating, and for good reason. Packed with fresh vegetables, fruits, proteins, and whole grains, salads provide essential nutrients, vitamins, and fiber.

- Balanced Nutrition: A well-crafted salad can include carbohydrates, proteins, healthy fats, and fiber, making it a complete and satisfying meal.

- Superfood Potential: Ingredients like kale, quinoa, nuts, and berries elevate the nutritional profile of salads, contributing to overall well-being.

2. A Canvas for Culinary Creativity

Salads are one of the most versatile dishes in the culinary world, offering endless opportunities for experimentation.

- Flavor Combinations: Sweet and savory, crunchy and creamy—salads are a playground for balancing textures and flavors.

- Global Inspiration: From a Thai papaya salad to a French Niçoise, salads can be infused with flavors from around the world.

- Innovative Presentations: Layered Mason jar salads, salad bowls, or plated salads can elevate the dining experience.

3. A Meal for Every Occasion

Salads can be tailored to fit any occasion, from light and refreshing summer lunches to hearty main courses for dinner.

- Casual Meals: Quick garden salads or protein-packed bowls are ideal for busy weeknights.

- Elegant Entertaining: Impress guests with artfully arranged salads featuring gourmet ingredients like edible flowers, burrata, or roasted figs.

- Seasonal Adaptability: Salads can be designed to highlight the freshest ingredients of each season, making them a year-round favorite.

The History and Evolution of Salads Across Cultures

1. Ancient Beginnings

The origins of salads trace back thousands of years, with ancient cultures incorporating raw vegetables and herbs into their diets.

- Ancient Rome and Greece: Early salads were simple mixtures of greens, herbs, and oils, often seasoned with salt or vinegar. These were seen as refreshing accompaniments to heavier dishes.

- Egypt: The use of onions, garlic, and leafy greens in Egyptian cuisine reflects the early beginnings of salad-like dishes.

2. The Renaissance of Salads

Salads gained popularity during the Renaissance in Europe, where elaborate vegetable arrangements became a symbol of sophistication and wealth.

- France: French chefs refined salads into composed dishes, adding ingredients like vinaigrettes and cheeses.

- Italy: Italians embraced the simplicity of fresh produce, with salads like Caprese showcasing minimal yet flavorful combinations.

3. Modern Global Influence

In the 20th and 21st centuries, salads became a global phenomenon, evolving into a category of their own with diverse cultural influences.

- United States: The Cobb and Caesar salads became iconic, combining fresh greens with hearty toppings and bold dressings.

- Middle East: Dishes like tabbouleh and fattoush highlight the region's use of grains, herbs, and tangy dressings.

- Asia: Salads like Thai green papaya and Japanese seaweed salad incorporate unique textures and bold flavors.

Tools, Ingredients, and Techniques for Exceptional Salads

1. Essential Tools

The right tools can make salad preparation more efficient and enjoyable.

- Salad Spinner: Removes excess water from greens, ensuring crispness.

- Sharp Knife: Essential for slicing vegetables, fruits, and proteins with precision.

- Mandoline: Creates uniform slices of vegetables for a professional presentation.

- Mixing Bowls: Useful for tossing salads and evenly coating ingredients with dressings.

- Tongs or Salad Servers: Ensures gentle handling of delicate greens and toppings.

2. Key Ingredients

The foundation of any great salad is its ingredients. Choose fresh, high-quality components to maximize flavor and nutrition.

Greens and Bases

- Leafy Greens: Romaine, arugula, spinach, kale, and mixed greens provide the base for most salads.

- Non-Leafy Bases: Grains like quinoa and farro, roasted vegetables, or even pasta can serve as hearty alternatives.

Proteins

- Meats and Seafood: Grilled chicken, shrimp, salmon, or steak.

- Plant-Based Options: Tofu, tempeh, chickpeas, or lentils.

Toppings and Add-Ins

- Crunchy Elements: Croutons, nuts, seeds, or crispy vegetables.

- Cheeses: Feta, goat cheese, Parmesan, or blue cheese for added creaminess and flavor.

- Fruits: Fresh or dried fruits like berries, apples, or cranberries for sweetness.

Dressings

- Classics: Ranch, Caesar, vinaigrettes, or balsamic glaze.

- Homemade Options: Lemon-tahini, miso-ginger, or avocado-lime dressings for a unique touch.

3. Techniques for Salad Success

Washing and Preparing Greens

- Always wash greens thoroughly and dry them with a salad spinner to prevent sogginess.

Balancing Flavors

- Incorporate elements of sweet, salty, tangy, and bitter to create a harmonious salad.

Layering Ingredients

- Start with the heaviest ingredients at the bottom and layer lighter elements on top for even distribution.

Tossing and Dressing

- Toss salads gently to avoid bruising delicate greens. Add dressing gradually to achieve the perfect coating without overwhelming the flavors.

Presentation Matters

- Arrange ingredients thoughtfully to create a visually appealing dish. Consider adding edible flowers or fresh herbs as garnishes.

Why Mastering Salad-Making Matters

Mastering the art of salad-making empowers you to create dishes that are as nourishing as they are delicious. Salads can transform a meal, serve as a blank canvas for creativity, and provide a sustainable way to celebrate the flavors of the season. Whether you're preparing a quick lunch or hosting an elaborate dinner, salads have the versatility to shine in any context.

This book will guide you through every aspect of salad-making, from understanding the basics to crafting show-stopping creations. As we explore recipes and techniques, you'll gain the confidence to experiment and create salads that reflect your personal taste and culinary flair.

The journey begins here, with a celebration of fresh ingredients, bold flavors, and the endless possibilities of the humble yet extraordinary salad.

Chapter 1: Greens and Bases

A great salad starts with a solid foundation, and the base you choose sets the tone for the flavors, textures, and nutritional profile of the dish. While greens are often the go-to for many salads, there is a world of non-leafy bases—like grains, pasta, and root vegetables—that can elevate your creations and provide variety. In this chapter, we'll explore the different types of greens and non-leafy bases, and learn how to choose the perfect foundation for your salad, whether it's light and refreshing or hearty and satisfying.

Exploring Different Types of Greens

Greens are the cornerstone of many salads, offering freshness, crunch, and a range of flavors that can be sweet, peppery, or slightly bitter. Choosing the right greens is essential for creating a balanced and flavorful salad. Here's a closer look at some of the most popular options:

1. Romaine Lettuce

- Texture and Flavor: Crisp and mild, with a slightly sweet flavor.

- Best Uses: Ideal for classic salads like Caesar, or as a crunchy base for protein-packed salads.

- Nutritional Benefits: A good source of vitamin C, vitamin K, and folate.

2. Arugula

- Texture and Flavor: Delicate leaves with a peppery bite.

- Best Uses: Great for adding a spicy note to mixed green salads or pairing with sweet fruits like pears or apples.

- Nutritional Benefits: High in calcium, potassium, and antioxidants.

3. Kale

- Texture and Flavor: Sturdy, fibrous leaves with a slightly bitter taste.

- Best Uses: Perfect for massaged salads, as it holds up well to heavy dressings and toppings.

- Nutritional Benefits: Rich in vitamins A, C, and K, as well as iron and fiber.

4. Spinach

- Texture and Flavor: Tender and slightly sweet with a hint of earthiness.

- Best Uses: Works well in both raw salads and wilted applications, like warm spinach salads.

- Nutritional Benefits: Packed with iron, magnesium, and vitamin C.

5. Mixed Greens

- Texture and Flavor: A blend of different greens, often including spinach, arugula, and baby lettuces.

- Best Uses: Versatile and ready-to-use for a variety of salads.

- Nutritional Benefits: Combines the benefits of multiple greens.

6. Butter Lettuce (Boston or Bibb)

- Texture and Flavor: Soft, buttery leaves with a mild flavor.

- Best Uses: Excellent for delicate salads with light dressings or as a wrap for fillings.

- Nutritional Benefits: A good source of vitamin A and potassium.

7. Endive and Radicchio

- Texture and Flavor: Endive offers crisp, slightly bitter leaves, while radicchio is firm with a sharp, bitter flavor.

- Best Uses: Perfect for adding a contrasting bite to salads or as a decorative edible bowl.

- Nutritional Benefits: High in fiber and antioxidants.

8. Watercress

- Texture and Flavor: Small, delicate leaves with a peppery flavor.

- Best Uses: Adds a punch of flavor to mixed salads or pairs beautifully with citrus fruits.

- Nutritional Benefits: A powerhouse of vitamin C and calcium.

Non-Leafy Bases: Expanding the Salad Horizon

While leafy greens are traditional, non-leafy bases can transform a salad into a hearty, filling meal. These options bring unique textures, flavors, and nutritional profiles to the table:

1. Grains

- Quinoa: A protein-rich, gluten-free grain with a nutty flavor. Perfect for grain bowls or Mediterranean-inspired salads.

- Farro: A chewy, hearty grain that pairs well with roasted vegetables and tangy dressings.

- Barley: Adds a nutty, chewy texture to salads and works well in warm or cold preparations.

- Brown Rice: A versatile base that absorbs flavors beautifully and adds bulk to salads.

2. Pasta

- Orzo: A rice-shaped pasta that's ideal for light, lemony pasta salads.

- Bowties and Rotini: These shapes hold onto dressings and toppings, making them excellent for hearty pasta salads.

- Gluten-Free Pasta: Options like lentil or chickpea pasta provide additional protein and fiber.

3. Root Vegetables

- Beets: Roasted or pickled, beets add sweetness and a pop of color.

- Sweet Potatoes: Roasted sweet potatoes bring warmth and creaminess.

- Carrots: Shredded raw carrots add crunch, while roasted carrots offer sweetness.

4. Legumes

- Chickpeas: High in protein and fiber, chickpeas are versatile and work well in Mediterranean salads.

- Lentils: Add earthy flavor and a soft texture, ideal for grain and vegetable-based salads.

- Black Beans: Perfect for Tex-Mex-inspired salads with avocado and lime dressing.

5. Fruits

- Fresh Fruits: Sliced apples, pears, or berries add sweetness and contrast to savory salads.

- Dried Fruits: Raisins, cranberries, and figs bring chewy texture and concentrated sweetness.

6. Other Unique Bases

- Cabbage: Shredded raw cabbage is perfect for slaws, while sautéed cabbage works in warm salads.

- Zoodles: Spiralized zucchini noodles are a low-carb alternative to pasta.

How to Choose the Right Base for Your Salad

1. Consider the Occasion

   - Light Salads: Use delicate greens like arugula or butter lettuce for simple starters or side dishes.

   - Hearty Salads: Opt for kale, grains, or pasta for main-course salads that need to satisfy.

   2. Balance Flavors and Textures

   - Combine multiple bases to create contrast:

   - Pair tender spinach with crunchy quinoa.

   - Mix sweet roasted beets with earthy lentils.

   3. Match the Dressing to the Base

   - Delicate Bases: Pair lighter dressings like vinaigrettes with tender greens.

   - Hearty Bases: Use creamy or robust dressings with kale, grains, or pasta.

   4. Keep Nutrition in Mind

   - Add nutrient-dense bases like kale, spinach, or quinoa to boost the health benefits of your salad.

   5. Seasonal Availability

   - Choose ingredients that are in season for the freshest flavor and best texture:

   - Spring: Tender greens, asparagus, and peas.

   - Summer: Tomatoes, cucumbers, and corn.

   - Fall: Squash, kale, and apples.

   - Winter: Root vegetables, hearty greens, and grains.

Tips for Preparing Greens and Bases

1. Washing and Storing Greens

   - Rinse greens thoroughly to remove dirt and pesticides.

   - Use a salad spinner to dry greens completely.

   - Store in a container lined with paper towels to keep greens crisp.

   2. Cooking Non-Leafy Bases

   - Grains and legumes should be cooked to the correct texture—tender but not mushy.

- Roast or grill vegetables to caramelize their natural sugars and enhance flavor.

3. Prepping for Easy Assembly

- Prepare bases in advance and store them separately to maintain freshness.

- Combine greens and toppings just before serving to prevent wilting.

Conclusion: The Foundation of a Great Salad

The base of a salad is more than just a starting point—it's the heart of the dish. Whether you're crafting a light, refreshing appetizer or a robust main course, the right greens or non-leafy bases can elevate your salad to new heights. By understanding the unique qualities of each option and experimenting with combinations, you can create salads that are as diverse as they are delicious.

In the next chapter, we'll dive into the world of dressings and vinaigrettes, the essential elements that bring your greens and bases to life, ensuring every bite is packed with flavor.

Chapter 2: Dressings and Vinaigrettes

Dressings and vinaigrettes are the soul of a great salad. They don't just add flavor; they bring cohesion, transforming a collection of ingredients into a harmonious dish. The perfect dressing can elevate even the simplest greens into something extraordinary, while an imbalanced one can overwhelm or mute the natural flavors of the salad's components. In this chapter, we'll explore why dressings are so essential, provide recipes for classic dressings, and delve into the art of balancing flavors to create your own signature dressings.

The Importance of a Good Dressing

1. Enhancing Flavor

Dressings amplify the natural flavors of salad ingredients by adding complementary notes of acidity, sweetness, or richness.

- Example: A tangy vinaigrette brings brightness to earthy greens like kale, while a creamy dressing like ranch balances the crunch of fresh vegetables.

2. Adding Moisture and Texture

The consistency of a dressing—whether light and silky or thick and creamy—provides an essential textural contrast to the salad.

- Silky: A well-emulsified vinaigrette clings to each leaf, delivering flavor in every bite.

- Creamy: Thicker dressings, like Caesar, coat ingredients for a luxurious mouthfeel.

3. Binding Ingredients Together

A good dressing unites disparate ingredients, ensuring the salad feels like a cohesive dish rather than a collection of random components.

- Example: The umami-rich flavors of Caesar dressing tie together romaine lettuce, croutons, and Parmesan cheese.

4. Personalization

Homemade dressings allow you to tailor flavors to your preferences or dietary needs. Whether you prefer tangy, sweet, or spicy, the possibilities are endless.

Recipes for Classic Dressings

1. Classic Vinaigrette

A vinaigrette is the foundation of many salads, striking the perfect balance between acidity and oil.

Ingredients:
- 1/4 cup extra-virgin olive oil
- 2 tablespoons red wine vinegar
- 1 teaspoon Dijon mustard
- 1 teaspoon honey (optional)
- Salt and pepper to taste

Instructions:
1. Combine vinegar, mustard, and honey in a bowl.
2. Slowly whisk in olive oil until emulsified.
3. Season with salt and pepper to taste.

Variations:
- Add minced garlic or shallots for extra depth.
- Swap red wine vinegar for balsamic, apple cider, or champagne vinegar.

2. Ranch Dressing

Creamy, tangy, and versatile, ranch dressing pairs well with fresh veggies, hearty greens, and even as a dip.

Ingredients:
- 1/2 cup mayonnaise
- 1/2 cup sour cream or Greek yogurt
- 1/4 cup buttermilk (adjust for desired consistency)
- 1 teaspoon garlic powder
- 1 teaspoon onion powder
- 1 tablespoon fresh parsley, chopped
- 1 tablespoon fresh dill, chopped
- Salt and pepper to taste

Instructions:

1. Whisk together mayonnaise, sour cream, and buttermilk.

2. Add garlic powder, onion powder, and herbs.

3. Season with salt and pepper. Adjust consistency with more buttermilk if needed.

3. Caesar Dressing

Rich and bold, Caesar dressing is a must for the iconic Caesar salad.

Ingredients:

- 2 anchovy fillets (or 1 teaspoon anchovy paste)
- 1 garlic clove, minced
- 1 tablespoon Dijon mustard
- 1 teaspoon Worcestershire sauce
- 1 tablespoon lemon juice
- 1/2 cup mayonnaise
- 1/4 cup grated Parmesan cheese
- Salt and pepper to taste

Instructions:

1. Mash anchovies and garlic into a paste using a mortar and pestle or the back of a spoon.

2. Mix in mustard, Worcestershire sauce, and lemon juice.

3. Whisk in mayonnaise and Parmesan cheese until smooth.

4. Season with salt and pepper.

Pro Tip: For a lighter version, substitute Greek yogurt for mayonnaise.

4. Honey Mustard Dressing

Sweet, tangy, and slightly spicy, this dressing works well with salads featuring chicken, bacon, or fruit.

Ingredients:

- 1/4 cup Dijon mustard
- 1/4 cup honey
- 2 tablespoons apple cider vinegar
- 1/4 cup olive oil
- Salt and pepper to taste

Instructions:

1. Whisk together mustard, honey, and vinegar.
2. Slowly add olive oil while whisking to emulsify.
3. Season with salt and pepper.

5. Balsamic Vinaigrette

A slightly sweet vinaigrette that pairs beautifully with greens, fruits, and nuts.
Ingredients:
- 1/4 cup balsamic vinegar
- 1/2 cup olive oil
- 1 teaspoon Dijon mustard
- 1 teaspoon honey or maple syrup
- Salt and pepper to taste
Instructions:
1. Combine vinegar, mustard, and honey in a bowl.
2. Slowly whisk in olive oil until emulsified.
3. Season with salt and pepper.

How to Balance Flavors in Homemade Dressings

Creating a balanced dressing requires attention to five key flavor elements: acidity, sweetness, saltiness, bitterness, and umami.

1. Acidity
Acidity provides brightness and balance to rich or earthy salad ingredients.
- Examples: Vinegars (red wine, apple cider, balsamic), citrus juices (lemon, lime).
- Tip: Start with a small amount and adjust based on your taste preferences.
2. Sweetness
Sweetness counters acidity and bitterness, creating a harmonious dressing.
- Examples: Honey, maple syrup, fruit purees, or even a pinch of sugar.
- Tip: Use natural sweeteners to add depth and complexity.
3. Saltiness

Salt enhances the flavors of other ingredients and provides a savory note.

- Examples: Kosher salt, soy sauce, or anchovy paste.

- Tip: Season incrementally to avoid overpowering the dressing.

4. Bitterness

Bitterness adds complexity, particularly in creamy or sweet dressings.

- Examples: Dijon mustard, arugula, or bitter greens blended into the dressing.

5. Umami

Umami brings depth and richness to dressings, making them more satisfying.

- Examples: Parmesan cheese, miso, Worcestershire sauce, or anchovies.

Tips for Perfecting Your Dressings

1. Use High-Quality Ingredients
    - Oils: Choose extra-virgin olive oil or avocado oil for superior flavor.
    - Vinegars: Opt for aged balsamic or artisanal vinegars for richer taste.
    2. Master Emulsification

To achieve a silky, cohesive dressing, whisk the oil into the acidic base slowly and steadily.

    3. Adjust Consistency

For thinner dressings, add water or citrus juice. For thicker ones, incorporate Greek yogurt or avocado.

    4. Store Properly

- In the Fridge: Most homemade dressings can be refrigerated for up to a week.

- Shake Before Use: Oil-based dressings may separate, so always shake before serving.

    5. Taste and Adjust

Taste as you go to ensure the right balance of flavors. A small adjustment can make all the difference.

Creative Additions to Dressings

1. Fresh Herbs
   - Basil, cilantro, parsley, or dill can add brightness and complexity.
2. Spices and Seasonings
   - Add paprika, cumin, or chili flakes for a kick of flavor.
3. Dairy
   - Greek yogurt, buttermilk, or crumbled blue cheese create creamy textures.
4. Nuts and Seeds
   - Blended almonds, tahini, or sesame seeds add richness.

Conclusion: Dressings as the Heart of a Salad

Dressings are the unsung heroes of salads, transforming simple ingredients into extraordinary dishes. By mastering the art of balancing flavors and experimenting with classic and custom recipes, you can elevate your salads to new heights. Whether you prefer a zesty vinaigrette or a luxurious creamy dressing, the possibilities are endless when you make them from scratch.

As we move to the next chapter, we'll explore how texture plays a vital role in creating satisfying salads, from the crunch of croutons to the creaminess of avocados. With the right dressing as your foundation, you're well on your way to crafting salads that are as delicious as they are memorable.

Chapter 3: Adding Texture

Texture is the unsung hero of a great salad. While flavors often take the spotlight, the textural elements—the crunch of nuts, the creaminess of avocado, or the chewiness of dried fruits—can transform an ordinary salad into a memorable dish. The right combination of textures adds complexity, interest, and satisfaction to every bite.

This chapter dives into the importance of texture in salads, explores a variety of ingredients that can elevate your creations, and provides practical DIY tips for making your own salad toppers. By the end, you'll have the tools and inspiration to craft salads that excite the palate and engage the senses.

The Role of Texture in Salads

1. Enhancing the Eating Experience

Texture contributes to the overall sensory experience, making salads more enjoyable to eat.

- Crunch: Adds excitement and contrast to softer ingredients like lettuce or creamy dressings.

- Creaminess: Provides a luxurious mouthfeel that balances sharp or acidic flavors.

- Chewiness: Offers substance and depth, creating a more satisfying meal.

2. Creating Balance

A well-balanced salad combines different textures to keep each bite interesting.

- Example: A Caesar salad blends the crunch of croutons with the creaminess of Parmesan and the crispness of romaine.

3. Highlighting Ingredients

Textural contrasts can showcase the unique qualities of individual ingredients, allowing each to shine in its own way.

- Example: Adding toasted nuts to a spinach salad not only enhances crunch but also complements the leafy greens' tender texture.

Ingredients That Add Texture

A variety of ingredients can enhance the texture of a salad, from common staples to unique additions. Here's a breakdown by category:

1. Crunchy Elements

Crunch provides an exciting contrast to soft or tender components.
- Nuts:
- Almonds, pecans, walnuts, cashews, pistachios.
- Toast or candy them for added flavor.
- Seeds:
- Sunflower seeds, pumpkin seeds, sesame seeds, chia seeds.
- Use raw or toasted for extra crunch.
- Croutons:
- Classic cubes of toasted bread, seasoned with herbs and spices.
- Try alternatives like tortilla strips or pita chips.
- Raw Vegetables:
- Shredded carrots, sliced radishes, cucumbers, or bell peppers.

2. Creamy Components

Creaminess adds a luxurious quality to salads, balancing acidic or spicy flavors.
- Cheese:
- Goat cheese, feta, blue cheese, ricotta, or burrata.
- Crumble, slice, or dollop for varying levels of creaminess.
- Avocado:
- Sliced, diced, or mashed into a dressing.

- Adds richness and healthy fats.
- Dressings:
- Creamy options like ranch, Caesar, or tahini-based dressings.
- Eggs:
- Soft-boiled, poached, or hard-boiled eggs provide creaminess and protein.

3. Chewy Additions

Chewy ingredients add substance and depth, making salads more filling.
- Dried Fruits:
- Cranberries, apricots, figs, raisins, or cherries.
- Their natural sweetness balances savory or tangy elements.
- Cooked Grains:
- Quinoa, farro, barley, or rice offer a satisfying chew.
- Proteins:
- Grilled chicken, shrimp, steak, or tempeh add a chewy, meaty texture.
- Legumes:
- Lentils, chickpeas, or black beans are soft yet substantial.

4. Crispy and Light

Light, crispy elements provide an airy contrast to heavier components.
- Fried Shallots or Onions:
- Adds a salty, savory crunch.
- Crispy Prosciutto or Bacon:
- Thin and crisp, these add a smoky, savory element.
- Rice Noodles or Wonton Strips:
- Crispy fried noodles add a satisfying crunch to Asian-inspired salads.

5. Unique and Gourmet Options

Elevate your salads with gourmet textural elements.
- Edible Flowers:
- Nasturtiums or pansies add a delicate crunch and visual appeal.
- Shaved Vegetables:
- Raw asparagus, fennel, or zucchini ribbons for subtle crunch.
- Grated or Fried Cheese:

- Parmesan crisps or grated Pecorino provide salty, crispy texture.

DIY Tips for Making Your Own Salad Toppers

Creating your own salad toppers is a fun and rewarding way to personalize your salads. Here are some simple techniques:

1. Homemade Croutons

Transform stale bread into crispy, flavorful croutons.

Ingredients:
- Bread (ciabatta, sourdough, or baguette)
- Olive oil
- Garlic powder, herbs (thyme, rosemary), salt, and pepper

Instructions:
1. Preheat oven to 375°F (190°C).
2. Cut bread into cubes and toss with olive oil and seasonings.
3. Spread on a baking sheet and bake for 10-15 minutes, flipping halfway through.
4. Cool and store in an airtight container.

Pro Tip: Experiment with different breads and spices for unique flavors.

2. Toasted Nuts and Seeds

Enhance the flavor and crunch of nuts and seeds by toasting them.

Ingredients:
- Nuts or seeds of your choice
- Olive oil (optional)
- Salt or spices for seasoning

Instructions:
1. Heat a dry skillet over medium heat.
2. Add nuts or seeds, stirring frequently, until golden and fragrant (3-5 minutes).
3. Let cool before using or storing.

Pro Tip: Toss seeds with tamari or smoked paprika before toasting for added depth.

3. Candied Nuts

Add a sweet, crunchy element to your salads with candied nuts.

Ingredients:
- 1 cup nuts (pecans, almonds, or walnuts)
- 1/4 cup sugar
- 2 tablespoons water

Instructions:
1. Heat sugar and water in a skillet over medium heat until dissolved.
2. Add nuts and stir to coat.
3. Cook until sugar crystallizes and nuts are evenly coated (5-7 minutes).
4. Spread on parchment paper to cool.

4. Crispy Shallots

Fried shallots add a savory, crispy topping to salads.

Ingredients:
- 2 large shallots, thinly sliced
- 1/2 cup vegetable oil

Instructions:
1. Heat oil in a skillet over medium heat.
2. Add shallots and fry until golden brown (3-4 minutes).
3. Remove with a slotted spoon and drain on paper towels.

5. Parmesan Crisps

Thin, crispy cheese crisps are a delicious addition to Caesar salads or gourmet greens.

Ingredients:
- Grated Parmesan cheese

Instructions:
1. Preheat oven to 400°F (200°C).
2. Place small mounds of grated cheese on a parchment-lined baking sheet.
3. Flatten slightly and bake for 5-7 minutes until golden.

4. Let cool and store in an airtight container.

How to Combine Textures for the Perfect Salad

Achieving a balance of textures requires intentional layering and thoughtful ingredient choices.

1. Start with a Base

- Choose a green or grain that provides the primary texture.

2. Add Layers

- Introduce contrasting textures, like creamy avocado, crunchy nuts, and chewy dried fruit.

3. Finish with a Crunch

- Sprinkle crispy toppings like croutons or fried shallots just before serving to maintain their texture.

Final Thoughts on Texture in Salads

Texture is the secret ingredient that elevates a salad from good to great. By understanding the role of crunch, creaminess, and chewiness, and using the tips and recipes in this chapter, you can create salads that are as exciting to eat as they are flavorful.

In the next chapter, we'll explore the importance of proteins in salads, from grilled meats to plant-based options, and how to incorporate them seamlessly into your creations. Together, these elements will help you build salads that are truly satisfying and unforgettable.

Chapter 4: Perfect Proteins

A salad becomes a complete and satisfying meal when paired with the right protein. Whether it's the tenderness of grilled chicken, the brininess of seared shrimp, the creaminess of soft-boiled eggs, or the earthiness of roasted chickpeas, proteins bring substance, flavor, and nutritional balance to your salad creations. The versatility of proteins means there's something for every dietary preference, from meat lovers to vegetarians, pescatarians, and vegans.

This chapter explores a variety of proteins suited to every diet, delves into techniques for preparing them to complement your salads, and provides practical tips for incorporating leftovers into your dishes. By the end, you'll feel confident adding the perfect protein to any salad, ensuring every bite is as satisfying as it is delicious.

Proteins for Every Diet

1. Meats

Meats are among the most popular protein choices for salads, offering robust flavors and textures.

- Chicken: Grilled, roasted, or shredded chicken is versatile and works with nearly any flavor profile.
- Beef: Thinly sliced steak or ground beef adds richness to hearty salads.
- Pork: Crispy bacon, pulled pork, or grilled tenderloin provide bold, savory notes.
- Turkey: Lean and flavorful, turkey works well in both warm and cold salads.

2. Seafood

Seafood adds a light, fresh quality to salads while being rich in protein and omega-3 fatty acids.

- Shrimp: Grilled, sautéed, or poached shrimp pair beautifully with citrus and avocado.
- Salmon: Flaky grilled or smoked salmon adds depth and richness.

- Tuna: Canned tuna is convenient, while fresh tuna steaks elevate gourmet salads.

- Crab and Lobster: These luxurious options are perfect for elegant occasions.

3. Plant-Based Proteins

Plant-based proteins are a staple for vegetarian and vegan diets, offering a range of flavors and textures.

- Tofu: Marinated and grilled or pan-fried tofu absorbs flavors beautifully.

- Tempeh: This fermented soybean product has a nutty flavor and firm texture.

- Legumes: Chickpeas, black beans, and lentils provide a hearty, earthy quality.

- Edamame: Young soybeans are a fresh, slightly sweet addition.

4. Eggs

Eggs are a simple yet satisfying protein source that complements many salads.

- Hard-Boiled Eggs: Perfect for Cobb salads or classic Niçoise salads.

- Soft-Boiled Eggs: The runny yolk adds creaminess and richness.

- Fried or Poached Eggs: These work beautifully on warm salads or grain bowls.

5. Dairy-Based Proteins

Cheese and yogurt bring both protein and creaminess to salads.

- Cheese: Options like feta, goat cheese, or Parmesan add bold flavors.

- Greek Yogurt: A base for dressings or dolloped on salads for tangy creaminess.

How to Prepare Proteins to Complement Your Salad

1. Chicken

Chicken is versatile and pairs well with a wide range of dressings and toppings.

- Grilled Chicken:
- Preparation: Marinate in olive oil, garlic, and herbs before grilling.
- Pairings: Caesar salads, Mediterranean salads, or Tex-Mex salads.
- Shredded Chicken:
- Preparation: Poach chicken breasts in broth with aromatics, then shred.
- Pairings: Add to taco salads or cold noodle salads.
- Roasted Chicken:
- Preparation: Roast a whole chicken with butter and herbs, then slice.
- Pairings: Works well in hearty grain salads or warm winter salads.

2. Beef

Beef adds richness and bold flavor to salads.
   - Steak:
   - Preparation: Grill or sear steak to medium-rare, let rest, then slice thinly.
   - Pairings: Combine with arugula, blue cheese, and balsamic vinaigrette for a steakhouse-style salad.
   - Ground Beef:
   - Preparation: Season with taco spices for Mexican-inspired salads or garlic and soy for Asian flavors.
   - Pairings: Use in taco salads or bowls with grains and veggies.

3. Seafood

Seafood brings a fresh, briny element to salads.
   - Shrimp:
   - Preparation: Marinate in garlic and lemon, then grill or sauté.
   - Pairings: Combine with avocado, citrus, and spinach for a light salad.
   - Salmon:
   - Preparation: Roast or grill with olive oil and herbs, or flake smoked salmon.
   - Pairings: Add to kale or mixed greens with a mustard vinaigrette.
   - Canned Tuna:
   - Preparation: Mix with olive oil, lemon juice, and capers for a Mediterranean twist.
   - Pairings: Add to Niçoise salads or pasta salads.

4. Plant-Based Proteins

Plant-based proteins shine with proper preparation and seasoning.
- Tofu:
- Preparation: Press tofu to remove excess water, then marinate and pan-fry or grill.
- Pairings: Works well with Asian-inspired salads featuring sesame or peanut dressing.
- Tempeh:
- Preparation: Steam to soften, then marinate and sauté or grill.
- Pairings: Combine with roasted vegetables and quinoa for a hearty salad.
- Legumes:
- Preparation: Use canned beans for convenience or cook dried beans for more flavor. Season with cumin, garlic, or lemon juice.
- Pairings: Perfect in grain salads or as a topping for greens.

5. Eggs

Eggs add richness and visual appeal to salads.
- Hard-Boiled Eggs:
- Preparation: Boil for 10 minutes, cool in ice water, and slice.
- Pairings: Use in Cobb salads or with smoked salmon and dill.
- Soft-Boiled Eggs:
- Preparation: Boil for 6 minutes, peel carefully, and serve halved.
- Pairings: Add to warm salads with roasted vegetables.

Tips for Incorporating Leftovers as Salad Proteins

Leftovers are an excellent way to add protein to salads while reducing food waste. Here's how to make the most of them:

1. Roast Chicken

Shred leftover roast chicken and toss with greens, nuts, and a light vinaigrette.

- Pro Tip: Use the bones to make a quick broth for a warm salad dressing.

2. Steak or Pork

Slice leftover steak or pork thinly and serve over arugula with a tangy dressing.

- Pro Tip: Warm slightly in a skillet for a comforting salad topping.

3. Seafood

Flake leftover salmon or shrimp and mix with grains and citrus for a fresh, light meal.

- Pro Tip: Combine with avocado and herbs for a seafood salad bowl.

4. Beans and Legumes

Use extra beans or lentils to bulk up a green salad or create a protein-rich grain bowl.

- Pro Tip: Toss with olive oil, lemon juice, and spices for extra flavor.

5. Cooked Eggs

Chop leftover boiled eggs and mix with greens, croutons, and a creamy dressing.

- Pro Tip: Add a dollop of leftover egg salad as a creamy protein topping.

Combining Proteins for Complex Salads

Mixing proteins can add depth and complexity to your salads.

- Example: Combine grilled chicken with crispy bacon and a soft-boiled egg for a Cobb-inspired salad.

- Vegetarian Combo: Pair roasted chickpeas with avocado and a dollop of hummus.

Conclusion: Building Perfectly Balanced Protein Salads

Proteins are the backbone of a satisfying salad, offering flavor, texture, and nourishment. By exploring different protein options and mastering preparation techniques, you can create salads that suit every dietary need and occasion. From leftover roast chicken to freshly grilled shrimp, the possibilities are endless—and delicious.

In the next chapter, we'll explore the art of incorporating fruits, nuts, and grains to create layered, multidimensional salads that delight the palate. Let's keep building salads that excite and satisfy.

Chapter 5: Simple Side Salads

Side salads are the quiet heroes of any meal. They add freshness, texture, and balance to the table, complementing main dishes without overshadowing them. Whether it's the crisp simplicity of a garden salad, the bold flavor of a classic Caesar, or the tangy crunch of coleslaw, side salads are versatile and easy to prepare. With the right techniques and thoughtful pairings, these humble accompaniments can elevate any dining experience.

This chapter focuses on creating fresh, flavorful side salads, provides quick techniques for preparation, and offers practical tips for pairing salads with various main dishes. By the end, you'll have a repertoire of simple yet impressive side salads that can seamlessly enhance any meal.

Why Side Salads Are Essential

1. They Add Freshness and Balance

Side salads bring a light, refreshing element that balances heavier main courses.

- Example: A tangy coleslaw cuts through the richness of barbecued meats, while a crisp garden salad complements a creamy pasta dish.

2. They Enhance the Nutritional Profile of a Meal

Including a side salad ensures that greens, vegetables, and other nutrient-dense ingredients are part of the meal.

3. They're Quick and Easy to Prepare

Side salads require minimal ingredients and preparation, making them a convenient addition to any meal.

Recipes for Simple Side Salads

1. Garden Salad

A garden salad is the epitome of simplicity—fresh greens and vegetables tossed with a light dressing.

Ingredients (Serves 4):
- 4 cups mixed greens (romaine, arugula, spinach)
- 1 cup cherry tomatoes, halved
- 1 cucumber, thinly sliced
- 1/4 red onion, thinly sliced
- 1/2 cup shredded carrots
- 1/4 cup olive oil
- 2 tablespoons red wine vinegar
- 1 teaspoon Dijon mustard
- Salt and pepper to taste

Instructions:

1. Prepare the Vegetables: Wash and dry the greens thoroughly. Slice the tomatoes, cucumber, onion, and carrots.

2. Make the Dressing: Whisk together olive oil, red wine vinegar, Dijon mustard, salt, and pepper.

3. Assemble the Salad: In a large bowl, combine the greens and vegetables. Drizzle with dressing and toss gently.

4. Serve: Garnish with croutons or seeds if desired.

Pro Tip: Add variety with seasonal vegetables like radishes, bell peppers, or avocado.

2. Classic Caesar Salad

The Caesar salad is a timeless favorite, known for its bold dressing, crisp romaine, and crunchy croutons.

Ingredients (Serves 4):
- 4 cups romaine lettuce, chopped
- 1/4 cup grated Parmesan cheese
- 1 cup croutons
- 1/4 cup Caesar dressing (see Chapter 2 for recipe)

Instructions:

1. Prepare the Lettuce: Wash, dry, and chop the romaine into bite-sized pieces.

2. Assemble the Salad: In a large bowl, combine romaine, Parmesan, and croutons.

3. Add Dressing: Toss with Caesar dressing until evenly coated.

4. Serve: Top with additional Parmesan if desired.

Pro Tip: For a gourmet touch, add grilled chicken or anchovies.

3. Coleslaw

Coleslaw is a versatile side salad with a tangy, creamy dressing and a satisfying crunch.

Ingredients (Serves 4):

- 2 cups shredded green cabbage

- 1 cup shredded purple cabbage

- 1 cup shredded carrots

- 1/4 cup mayonnaise

- 1 tablespoon apple cider vinegar

- 1 teaspoon sugar

- Salt and pepper to taste

Instructions:

1. Prepare the Vegetables: Shred the cabbage and carrots using a knife, box grater, or food processor.

2. Make the Dressing: Whisk together mayonnaise, apple cider vinegar, sugar, salt, and pepper.

3. Combine: Toss the vegetables with the dressing until evenly coated.

4. Serve: Chill in the refrigerator for at least 30 minutes before serving.

Pro Tip: Add a teaspoon of Dijon mustard or celery seeds for extra flavor.

Quick Techniques for Preparing Fresh, Flavorful Sides

1. Invest in Quality Ingredients

- Use the freshest vegetables and greens to ensure vibrant flavors and textures.

- Choose high-quality olive oil and vinegars for dressings.

2. Properly Wash and Dry Greens

- Rinse greens thoroughly to remove dirt and pesticides.

- Dry them completely with a salad spinner or clean kitchen towel to prevent sogginess.

3. Chop Vegetables Uniformly

- Slice vegetables thinly and evenly for better presentation and ease of eating.

- Use a mandoline for precise cuts.

4. Balance Flavors

- Aim for a combination of flavors: sweet (carrots, tomatoes), tangy (vinaigrette, citrus), and savory (cheese, croutons).

5. Toss Just Before Serving

- Dress salads only when ready to serve to keep greens crisp and fresh.

Tips for Pairing Side Salads with Main Dishes

Pairing side salads with main dishes is an art that considers flavors, textures, and themes.

1. Balance Richness

- Pair creamy or heavy dishes with light, acidic salads.

- Example: A garden salad with lemon vinaigrette balances creamy pasta.

2. Complement Flavors

- Match bold flavors with equally assertive salads.

- Example: Serve a Caesar salad alongside grilled steak for a classic pairing.

3. Consider the Cuisine

- Align the salad with the cuisine of the main dish.

- Example: Pair coleslaw with American barbecue or a Greek salad with Mediterranean dishes.

4. Play with Textures
 - Complement soft or tender dishes with crunchy salads.
 - Example: A crisp coleslaw contrasts with tender pulled pork.
5. Keep It Simple
 - Let the salad enhance, not compete with, the main dish.
 - Example: A lightly dressed green salad works well with elaborate mains like coq au vin.

Creative Variations for Side Salads

1. Garden Salad Variations
  - Add sliced avocado, roasted beets, or goat cheese for a gourmet twist.
  2. Caesar Salad Variations
 - Use kale or mixed greens instead of romaine for a modern take.
 - Add grilled shrimp or tofu for extra protein.
 3. Coleslaw Variations
 - Swap mayonnaise for Greek yogurt for a lighter version.
 - Add chopped apples or raisins for sweetness.

Conclusion: The Versatility of Simple Side Salads

Side salads are more than an afterthought—they're a vital part of a well-rounded meal. With the recipes and techniques in this chapter, you can create fresh, flavorful salads that pair beautifully with any dish. Whether it's a classic Caesar, a vibrant garden salad, or a tangy coleslaw, these simple sides will enhance your meals and delight your guests.

In the next chapter, we'll explore hearty main-course salads that are satisfying enough to take center stage. With the foundation of side salads mastered, you're ready to dive into the heartier world of salads as meals.

Chapter 6: Hearty Main Course Salads

Salads are no longer confined to the sidelines of the culinary world. Hearty main course salads have emerged as satisfying, nutrient-dense meals that combine robust flavors, diverse textures, and filling ingredients. With the right mix of proteins, grains, vegetables, and dressings, salads can take center stage on your table and provide a meal that is both delicious and nourishing.

This chapter explores classic main course salads such as the Cobb salad, chicken Caesar, and grain bowl salads. You'll learn how to balance flavors and textures to create a harmonious dish, as well as techniques for making salads more filling and nutrient-dense without sacrificing taste.

Why Main Course Salads?

1. Versatility

Main course salads can be tailored to any dietary preference or occasion. They are equally suited for quick weeknight dinners, elegant brunches, or lunch meal prep.

2. Balanced Nutrition

A well-designed main course salad provides a complete meal, offering protein, healthy fats, fiber, and carbohydrates.

3. Endless Creativity

From global flavors to seasonal ingredients, the possibilities for main course salads are limitless.

Recipes for Hearty Main Course Salads

1. Cobb Salad

The Cobb salad is a classic American dish that combines a variety of ingredients for a colorful, satisfying meal.

Ingredients (Serves 4):
- 6 cups chopped romaine lettuce
- 2 cooked chicken breasts, diced
- 4 hard-boiled eggs, quartered
- 1 avocado, sliced
- 1 cup cherry tomatoes, halved
- 1/2 cup crumbled blue cheese
- 4 slices cooked bacon, crumbled
- 1/4 cup chives, chopped (optional)
- 1/2 cup red wine vinaigrette or ranch dressing

Instructions:

1. Prepare Ingredients: Wash and chop romaine lettuce. Dice chicken, cook and crumble bacon, and slice avocado.

2. Assemble the Salad: In a large serving bowl or platter, arrange the lettuce as a base. Top with rows of chicken, eggs, avocado, cherry tomatoes, blue cheese, and bacon.

3. Dress and Serve: Drizzle with dressing and garnish with chives. Serve immediately.

Pro Tip: Swap blue cheese for feta or goat cheese for a milder flavor.

2. Chicken Caesar Salad

The chicken Caesar salad is a protein-packed version of the classic Caesar, featuring tender grilled chicken for added substance.

Ingredients (Serves 4):
- 6 cups chopped romaine lettuce
- 2 cooked chicken breasts, sliced
- 1/4 cup grated Parmesan cheese
- 1 cup croutons
- 1/2 cup Caesar dressing (see Chapter 2 for recipe)

Instructions:

1. Prepare Ingredients: Wash and chop romaine lettuce. Slice grilled chicken.

2. Assemble the Salad: In a large bowl, combine romaine lettuce, Parmesan cheese, croutons, and chicken.

3. Add Dressing: Toss with Caesar dressing until evenly coated.

4. Serve: Top with additional Parmesan for garnish.

Pro Tip: Add a soft-boiled egg or anchovies for an authentic touch.

3. Grain Bowl Salad

Grain bowls are a modern twist on hearty salads, combining grains, proteins, and fresh vegetables in a single dish.

Ingredients (Serves 4):

- 2 cups cooked quinoa or farro

- 1 cup roasted sweet potatoes, diced

- 1 cup chickpeas, drained and rinsed

- 1 cup cherry tomatoes, halved

- 1 avocado, sliced

- 4 cups mixed greens (spinach, arugula, or kale)

- 1/4 cup feta cheese, crumbled

- 1/2 cup tahini dressing

Instructions:

1. Prepare Ingredients: Cook grains, roast sweet potatoes, and slice avocado.

2. Assemble the Bowl: In individual bowls, layer grains, greens, sweet potatoes, chickpeas, tomatoes, and avocado.

3. Add Dressing: Drizzle with tahini dressing and top with feta cheese.

4. Serve: Mix well before eating.

Pro Tip: Substitute grains with wild rice or couscous for variation.

Balancing Flavors and Textures

A successful main course salad combines flavors and textures to create a cohesive and satisfying dish.

1. Balance Flavors

- Sweet: Roasted sweet potatoes, dried cranberries, or fresh fruits.

- Savory: Grilled meats, roasted vegetables, or salty cheeses.
- Tangy: Citrus dressings, pickled onions, or balsamic glaze.
- Spicy: Crushed red pepper flakes, jalapeños, or spicy dressings.

2. Combine Textures
- Crunchy: Nuts, seeds, croutons, or raw vegetables.
- Creamy: Avocado, cheese, or dressings.
- Chewy: Cooked grains, beans, or dried fruits.

3. Use Contrasting Temperatures
- Pair warm proteins or roasted vegetables with cool, crisp greens for an engaging contrast.

Making Salads Filling and Nutrient-Dense

A main course salad should not only be delicious but also satisfying enough to serve as a complete meal. Here's how to make it happen:

1. Add Proteins
   Incorporate a substantial protein source to make the salad filling:
   - Animal Proteins: Grilled chicken, steak, salmon, or shrimp.
   - Plant Proteins: Tofu, tempeh, chickpeas, or lentils.

2. Include Healthy Fats
   Healthy fats enhance flavor and increase satiety:
   - Examples: Avocado, nuts, seeds, olive oil-based dressings.

3. Use Whole Grains
   Grains add texture, flavor, and complex carbohydrates for sustained energy:
   - Examples: Quinoa, farro, barley, or brown rice.

4. Incorporate Fiber-Rich Vegetables

Fiber keeps you full and supports digestion:
- Examples: Broccoli, kale, carrots, and Brussels sprouts.
5. Add Nutrient-Dense Toppings
Enhance your salad with superfoods:
- Examples: Chia seeds, hemp seeds, or nutritional yeast.

Quick Tips for Meal-Prepping Main Course Salads

1. Prep Ingredients in Advance
   - Wash and chop greens, cook grains, and prepare proteins ahead of time.
   2. Store Ingredients Separately
   - Keep dressings, proteins, and toppings separate until serving to maintain freshness.
   3. Use Airtight Containers
   - Layer salads in jars for portability and freshness. Place heavier ingredients at the bottom and greens at the top.
   4. Double Up
   - Cook extra grains, roast additional vegetables, or grill more proteins for multiple salads throughout the week.

Creative Variations for Hearty Salads

1. Mediterranean Salad
   Combine grilled chicken, cucumbers, tomatoes, feta, and olives with a lemon-oregano dressing.
   2. Asian-Inspired Bowl
   Layer sesame-marinated tofu, edamame, shredded carrots, and pickled ginger over soba noodles.
   3. Tex-Mex Salad
   Mix romaine lettuce with grilled steak, black beans, corn, avocado, and spicy chipotle dressing.
   4. Vegan Power Bowl
   Combine quinoa, kale, roasted sweet potatoes, chickpeas, and tahini dressing for a plant-based meal.

Conclusion: Elevating Salads to Main Course Status

Hearty main course salads are more than just meals—they're culinary experiences that combine flavor, texture, and nutrition in one bowl. With the recipes, techniques, and tips in this chapter, you can transform salads into satisfying and balanced meals that will delight your taste buds and fuel your body.

In the next chapter, we'll explore healthy and light salad options that are perfect for detoxing, weight management, or simply enjoying a lighter meal. Let's keep building salads that inspire and nourish.

Chapter 7: Healthy and Light Options

Healthy and light salads are perfect for those seeking nutrient-rich, refreshing meals that don't compromise on flavor. These salads are packed with superfoods, vibrant vegetables, whole grains, and lean proteins, offering a balanced mix of taste and nourishment. In this chapter, we'll explore recipes like Detox Kale Salad, Quinoa Salad, and Mediterranean Chickpea Salad, delve into the role of superfoods and nutrient-dense ingredients, and share strategies for keeping your salads both healthy and flavorful.

Why Choose Healthy and Light Salads?

1. Nutritional Benefits

Healthy salads incorporate a variety of whole, fresh ingredients, delivering essential vitamins, minerals, antioxidants, and fiber in every bite.

2. Weight Management

Light salads can be filling and satisfying without being calorie-dense, making them ideal for maintaining or losing weight.

3. Versatility

Healthy salads are easy to customize for different dietary preferences, including vegetarian, vegan, gluten-free, and low-carb.

Recipes for Healthy and Light Salads

1. Detox Kale Salad

This detoxifying salad combines nutrient-dense kale with fresh vegetables, seeds, and a zesty lemon dressing, making it perfect for resetting your body after indulgent meals.

Ingredients (Serves 4):

- 6 cups kale, chopped
- 1 cup shredded carrots
- 1 cup red cabbage, thinly sliced
- 1/2 cup pomegranate seeds
- 1/4 cup sunflower seeds
- 1 avocado, diced
- 1/4 cup lemon juice
- 2 tablespoons olive oil
- 1 teaspoon honey or maple syrup
- Salt and pepper to taste

Instructions:

1. Prepare the Kale: Remove kale stems and chop leaves. Massage with a pinch of salt to soften.

2. Assemble the Salad: In a large bowl, combine kale, carrots, cabbage, pomegranate seeds, sunflower seeds, and avocado.

3. Make the Dressing: Whisk together lemon juice, olive oil, honey, salt, and pepper.

4. Dress the Salad: Drizzle dressing over the salad and toss gently. Serve immediately.

Pro Tip: Add cooked quinoa or grilled chicken for extra protein.

2. Quinoa Salad

This light yet satisfying salad pairs fluffy quinoa with fresh vegetables, herbs, and a tangy vinaigrette for a well-rounded dish.

Ingredients (Serves 4):

- 1 cup quinoa, cooked and cooled
- 1 cup cherry tomatoes, halved
- 1 cucumber, diced
- 1/4 red onion, thinly sliced
- 1/4 cup fresh parsley, chopped
- 1/4 cup fresh mint, chopped
- 1/4 cup crumbled feta cheese (optional)
- 1/4 cup olive oil
- 3 tablespoons lemon juice

- 1 teaspoon Dijon mustard
- Salt and pepper to taste

Instructions:

1. Cook Quinoa: Rinse quinoa under cold water. Cook according to package instructions, then cool.

2. Combine Ingredients: In a large bowl, mix quinoa, tomatoes, cucumber, onion, parsley, mint, and feta cheese.

3. Make the Dressing: Whisk olive oil, lemon juice, Dijon mustard, salt, and pepper.

4. Toss and Serve: Pour dressing over the salad and toss gently. Serve chilled.

Pro Tip: Add chickpeas or grilled shrimp for a heartier version.

3. Mediterranean Chickpea Salad

This vibrant salad features the flavors of the Mediterranean, with chickpeas, fresh vegetables, and a zesty herb dressing.

Ingredients (Serves 4):

- 2 cups cooked or canned chickpeas, rinsed and drained
- 1 cup cherry tomatoes, halved
- 1 cucumber, diced
- 1/4 red onion, finely chopped
- 1/4 cup Kalamata olives, sliced
- 1/4 cup crumbled feta cheese
- 2 tablespoons fresh parsley, chopped
- 2 tablespoons fresh dill, chopped
- 3 tablespoons olive oil
- 2 tablespoons red wine vinegar
- 1 teaspoon dried oregano
- Salt and pepper to taste

Instructions:

1. Combine Ingredients: In a large bowl, mix chickpeas, tomatoes, cucumber, onion, olives, feta, parsley, and dill.

2. Make the Dressing: Whisk together olive oil, red wine vinegar, oregano, salt, and pepper.

3. Toss and Serve: Pour dressing over the salad and toss until well combined. Serve immediately or refrigerate.

Pro Tip: Serve with whole-grain pita or grilled chicken for a complete meal.

The Role of Superfoods and Nutrient-Dense Ingredients

Superfoods are ingredients that are exceptionally rich in nutrients, antioxidants, and health benefits. Incorporating them into salads enhances both their nutritional value and their flavor profiles.

1. Leafy Greens
- Examples: Kale, spinach, arugula, Swiss chard.
- Benefits: High in vitamins A, C, and K, as well as calcium, iron, and fiber.

2. Whole Grains
- Examples: Quinoa, farro, barley, bulgur.
- Benefits: Provide complex carbohydrates, fiber, and plant-based protein for sustained energy.

3. Seeds and Nuts
- Examples: Chia seeds, sunflower seeds, almonds, walnuts.
- Benefits: Rich in healthy fats, protein, and minerals like magnesium and zinc.

4. Fruits
- Examples: Berries, citrus, pomegranate seeds, apples.
- Benefits: Packed with antioxidants, vitamin C, and natural sweetness.

5. Healthy Fats
- Examples: Avocado, olive oil, tahini.
- Benefits: Support heart health and improve the absorption of fat-soluble vitamins.

6. Protein-Rich Additions
- Examples: Chickpeas, lentils, tofu, grilled chicken, or salmon.
- Benefits: Essential for muscle repair and overall satiety.

Strategies for Keeping Salads Healthy and Flavorful

1. Use Homemade Dressings

Store-bought dressings can be high in sugar, sodium, and unhealthy fats. Making your own allows you to control the ingredients and flavor.

2. Balance Flavors

- Combine sweet, savory, and tangy elements for a dynamic taste.

- Example: Pair sweet fruits like mango with salty feta and a tangy vinaigrette.

3. Incorporate a Variety of Textures

- Add crunch with nuts or seeds, creaminess with avocado, and chewiness with dried fruits or grains.

4. Focus on Whole Ingredients

- Use fresh, unprocessed ingredients to maximize nutrition and flavor.

- Avoid heavy, calorie-dense toppings like fried croutons or excessive cheese.

5. Add Herbs and Spices

- Fresh herbs like parsley, dill, mint, or cilantro add vibrancy.

- Spices like cumin, paprika, or turmeric boost flavor without adding calories.

6. Serve Smart Portions

- Keep an eye on portion sizes for calorie-dense ingredients like nuts, seeds, and cheese.

Creative Variations for Healthy Salads

1. Berry Spinach Salad

Combine spinach, strawberries, blueberries, and walnuts with a poppy seed dressing.

2. Thai Peanut Salad

Mix shredded cabbage, carrots, and edamame with a creamy peanut dressing.

3. Roasted Beet and Goat Cheese Salad

Layer arugula, roasted beets, goat cheese, and pistachios with a balsamic vinaigrette.

4. Sweet Potato and Lentil Salad
Toss roasted sweet potatoes, lentils, and kale with a lemon-tahini dressing.

Conclusion: Creating Healthy and Light Salads

Healthy and light salads are a celebration of vibrant, nutrient-dense ingredients that nourish the body and delight the palate. By incorporating superfoods, balancing flavors and textures, and using fresh, wholesome ingredients, you can create salads that are both satisfying and healthful. Whether it's a Detox Kale Salad, a Quinoa Salad, or a Mediterranean Chickpea Salad, these recipes offer endless possibilities for delicious meals.

In the next chapter, we'll explore how to bring global flavors into your salads, drawing inspiration from cuisines around the world to create unique and unforgettable dishes. Let's continue this journey toward building salads that excite and inspire.

Chapter 8: Mediterranean-Inspired Salads

Mediterranean cuisine is celebrated for its emphasis on fresh, wholesome ingredients and bold, vibrant flavors. Salads from this region are no exception, often combining crisp vegetables, fragrant herbs, and flavorful toppings like olives, feta, and citrus-based dressings. These salads are more than just dishes—they are expressions of a way of life that values health, simplicity, and community.

In this chapter, we'll explore three iconic Mediterranean-inspired salads: Greek Salad, Fattoush, and Tabbouleh. You'll learn how to recreate authentic Mediterranean flavors using key ingredients and techniques, ensuring your salads are both delicious and true to their origins.

The Essence of Mediterranean Salads

1. Fresh, Seasonal Ingredients

Mediterranean salads emphasize fresh, seasonal produce like tomatoes, cucumbers, peppers, and herbs. Using peak-season ingredients is essential for achieving the vibrant flavors this cuisine is known for.

2. Balance of Flavors

Mediterranean salads balance sweetness, tanginess, saltiness, and earthiness. This harmony is achieved through the thoughtful use of ingredients like citrus, olives, and cheese.

3. Simplicity and Elegance

These salads rely on simple preparations that allow individual ingredients to shine, with minimal cooking and maximum freshness.

Key Ingredients in Mediterranean Salads

1. Olives

- Varieties: Kalamata, green Castelvetrano, or black olives.

- Role: Add a salty, briny flavor that enhances the freshness of vegetables.

2. Feta Cheese

- Type: Traditionally made from sheep or goat's milk, feta is crumbly, tangy, and slightly creamy.

- Role: Adds richness and a savory note to salads.

3. Fresh Herbs

- Common Choices: Parsley, mint, dill, oregano, and basil.

- Role: Herbs bring freshness and aromatic complexity to Mediterranean dishes.

4. Citrus

- Examples: Lemons and oranges.

- Role: Add brightness and tanginess, often used in dressings or marinades.

5. Extra-Virgin Olive Oil

- Why It Matters: High-quality olive oil is the foundation of Mediterranean dressings, offering richness and a smooth, peppery flavor.

6. Vegetables

- Staples: Tomatoes, cucumbers, onions, peppers, and leafy greens.

- Role: These are the building blocks of Mediterranean salads, providing crunch, sweetness, and color.

Recipes for Mediterranean-Inspired Salads

1. Greek Salad

This classic salad combines crisp vegetables, briny olives, and creamy feta for a refreshing and satisfying dish.

Ingredients (Serves 4):

- 4 cups tomatoes, chopped

- 2 cups cucumbers, sliced

- 1 red onion, thinly sliced

- 1 green bell pepper, sliced

- 1/2 cup Kalamata olives

- 1/2 cup feta cheese, crumbled

- 1/4 cup extra-virgin olive oil
- 2 tablespoons red wine vinegar
- 1 teaspoon dried oregano
- Salt and pepper to taste

Instructions:

1. Prepare Vegetables: Wash and chop the tomatoes, cucumbers, onions, and bell pepper.

2. Assemble the Salad: Combine vegetables, olives, and feta in a large bowl.

3. Make the Dressing: Whisk together olive oil, red wine vinegar, oregano, salt, and pepper.

4. Dress the Salad: Drizzle dressing over the salad and toss gently. Serve immediately.

Pro Tip: Serve with warm pita bread or grilled chicken for a complete meal.

2. Fattoush

Fattoush is a Levantine bread salad that features crispy pita chips, fresh vegetables, and a tangy sumac dressing.

Ingredients (Serves 4):

- 2 pieces of pita bread, torn into small pieces
- 3 cups romaine lettuce, chopped
- 1 cup cherry tomatoes, halved
- 1 cucumber, diced
- 1/2 red onion, thinly sliced
- 1/4 cup fresh parsley, chopped
- 2 tablespoons fresh mint, chopped
- 1/4 cup lemon juice
- 1/4 cup olive oil
- 1 teaspoon sumac
- Salt and pepper to taste

Instructions:

1. Prepare the Pita Chips: Toast torn pita bread in a 375°F (190°C) oven for 10 minutes or until crispy.

2. Prepare Vegetables: Wash and chop romaine, tomatoes, cucumber, and onion.

3. Assemble the Salad: Combine vegetables, herbs, and pita chips in a large bowl.

4. Make the Dressing: Whisk together lemon juice, olive oil, sumac, salt, and pepper.

5. Dress and Serve: Toss salad with dressing and serve immediately.

Pro Tip: Add radishes or pomegranate seeds for extra color and flavor.

3. Tabbouleh

Tabbouleh is a parsley-forward salad with bulgur wheat, tomatoes, and cucumbers, offering a light yet hearty dish.

Ingredients (Serves 4):

- 1/2 cup bulgur wheat
- 1 cup parsley, finely chopped
- 1/4 cup fresh mint, finely chopped
- 1 cup tomatoes, diced
- 1 cucumber, diced
- 1/4 cup green onions, chopped
- 1/4 cup lemon juice
- 1/4 cup olive oil
- Salt and pepper to taste

Instructions:

1. Prepare Bulgur Wheat: Soak bulgur wheat in hot water for 10 minutes, then drain and cool.

2. Prepare Vegetables: Wash and finely chop parsley, mint, tomatoes, cucumber, and green onions.

3. Combine Ingredients: Mix bulgur, herbs, and vegetables in a large bowl.

4. Make the Dressing: Whisk together lemon juice, olive oil, salt, and pepper.

5. Dress and Serve: Toss salad with dressing and serve chilled.

Pro Tip: Use quinoa instead of bulgur for a gluten-free version.

How to Recreate Authentic Mediterranean Flavors

1. Use Fresh, High-Quality Ingredients
    - Fresh herbs, ripe vegetables, and premium olive oil are non-negotiable.
    2. Embrace Simplicity
    - Mediterranean salads rely on minimal ingredients and straightforward preparations.
    3. Highlight Key Ingredients
    - Use olives, feta, and fresh herbs liberally to capture the essence of Mediterranean cuisine.
    4. Balance Acidity and Oil
    - A perfect Mediterranean dressing balances the richness of olive oil with the tanginess of lemon or vinegar.
    5. Season Generously
    - Season salads with sea salt, black pepper, and spices like sumac, oregano, or za'atar for authenticity.

Pairing Mediterranean Salads with Main Dishes

1. Greek Salad
    - Pair with grilled lamb, chicken souvlaki, or baked fish.
    2. Fattoush
    - Serve alongside roasted vegetables, falafel, or a mezze platter.
    3. Tabbouleh
    - Complement with stuffed grape leaves, hummus, or grilled shrimp.

Creative Variations for Mediterranean Salads

1. Quinoa Greek Salad
    Substitute quinoa for a heartier version of the classic Greek salad.
    2. Fattoush with Chickpeas

Add chickpeas for extra protein and substance.

3. Pomegranate Tabbouleh

Incorporate pomegranate seeds for a burst of sweetness and color.

Conclusion: Celebrating Mediterranean Salads

Mediterranean-inspired salads are a celebration of freshness, flavor, and simplicity. By mastering these recipes and techniques, you can bring the spirit of the Mediterranean to your table, whether it's a light lunch or an elegant dinner. From the classic Greek Salad to the herbaceous Tabbouleh, these dishes are versatile, healthy, and utterly delicious.

In the next chapter, we'll explore Asian-inspired salads that offer bold, exciting flavors through the use of sesame, ginger, soy, and other iconic ingredients. Let's continue this global journey through salads!

Chapter 9: Asian-Inspired Salads

Asian-inspired salads are renowned for their bold flavors, vibrant colors, and unique textures. They masterfully balance sweet, salty, sour, and spicy elements to create dishes that excite the palate. With fresh ingredients like green papaya, sesame oil, miso, and ginger, these salads are as nourishing as they are flavorful. Whether you're crafting a zesty Thai green papaya salad, a hearty sesame chicken salad, or a delicate Japanese seaweed salad, these recipes will transport you to the heart of Asia.

This chapter explores how to create three iconic Asian-inspired salads, introduces signature ingredients, and shares tips for achieving the perfect balance of flavors. By the end, you'll have the tools and techniques to recreate these vibrant dishes with confidence.

The Essence of Asian-Inspired Salads

1. Balancing Flavors

Asian cuisine thrives on balance. Salads in this genre often incorporate contrasting flavors:
- Sweet: Honey, palm sugar, or fruit.
- Salty: Soy sauce, fish sauce, or miso.
- Sour: Lime juice, rice vinegar, or tamarind.
- Spicy: Chili peppers, chili oil, or sriracha.

2. Emphasis on Texture

Asian-inspired salads are a feast for the senses, combining crisp vegetables, tender proteins, chewy noodles, and crunchy nuts or seeds.

3. Health and Freshness

These salads are typically light and packed with fresh, raw, or lightly cooked ingredients, making them a nutritious addition to any meal.

Signature Ingredients in Asian-Inspired Salads

1. Soy Sauce

- Type: Light soy sauce for flavor, dark soy sauce for richness.
- Uses: Adds umami and saltiness to dressings and marinades.

2. Sesame Oil
- Flavor: Nutty and aromatic.
- Uses: Enhances dressings and brings depth to vegetable salads.

3. Miso
- Type: Fermented soybean paste, available in white, yellow, or red varieties.
- Uses: Adds savory richness to dressings and soups.

4. Ginger
- Flavor: Spicy and slightly sweet.
- Uses: A key ingredient in marinades, dressings, and pickled garnishes.

5. Fish Sauce
- Flavor: Salty and umami-rich.
- Uses: Found in Thai and Vietnamese salads for depth of flavor.

6. Rice Vinegar
- Flavor: Mild and slightly sweet.
- Uses: Adds acidity without overpowering the dish.

7. Chili Peppers
- Type: Fresh chilies, chili flakes, or chili oil.
- Uses: Introduces heat and spice to balance sweet and sour flavors.

Recipes for Asian-Inspired Salads

1. Thai Green Papaya Salad (Som Tum)

This refreshing salad combines the crunch of green papaya with the bold flavors of lime, fish sauce, and chili.

Ingredients (Serves 4):
- 2 cups shredded green papaya
- 1/2 cup cherry tomatoes, halved
- 1/2 cup green beans, cut into 2-inch pieces
- 1/4 cup roasted peanuts, crushed
- 1-2 Thai chilies, finely chopped (adjust to taste)
- 2 tablespoons fish sauce
- 2 tablespoons lime juice

- 1 tablespoon palm sugar (or brown sugar)
- 1 garlic clove, minced

Instructions:

1. Prepare the Papaya: Shred green papaya using a mandoline or box grater.

2. Make the Dressing: Whisk together fish sauce, lime juice, palm sugar, garlic, and chilies until the sugar dissolves.

3. Combine Ingredients: Toss papaya, tomatoes, and green beans in a large bowl.

4. Add Dressing: Pour dressing over the salad and toss gently.

5. Serve: Garnish with crushed peanuts and serve immediately.

Pro Tip: Add dried shrimp for an authentic Thai flavor.

2. Sesame Chicken Salad

This hearty salad pairs tender chicken with crisp vegetables and a rich sesame dressing.

Ingredients (Serves 4):

- 2 cooked chicken breasts, shredded
- 4 cups mixed greens (spinach, arugula, or romaine)
- 1 cup shredded carrots
- 1 cup red cabbage, thinly sliced
- 1/4 cup green onions, chopped
- 1/4 cup sesame seeds, toasted
- 1/4 cup soy sauce
- 2 tablespoons sesame oil
- 1 tablespoon rice vinegar
- 1 tablespoon honey
- 1 teaspoon ginger, grated

Instructions:

1. Prepare the Vegetables: Wash and chop greens, shred carrots, and slice cabbage.

2. Make the Dressing: Whisk together soy sauce, sesame oil, rice vinegar, honey, and ginger.

3. Assemble the Salad: In a large bowl, combine chicken, greens, carrots, cabbage, and green onions.

4. Add Dressing: Drizzle dressing over the salad and toss to combine.

5. Serve: Garnish with toasted sesame seeds.

Pro Tip: Add crispy wonton strips for extra crunch.

3. Japanese Seaweed Salad

This delicate salad highlights the umami flavors of seaweed, sesame, and soy.

Ingredients (Serves 4):

- 1 cup dried wakame seaweed
- 1 tablespoon soy sauce
- 1 tablespoon rice vinegar
- 1 teaspoon sesame oil
- 1 teaspoon mirin (optional)
- 1/2 teaspoon ginger, grated
- 1/4 teaspoon chili flakes
- 1 tablespoon sesame seeds, toasted

Instructions:

1. Rehydrate Seaweed: Soak dried wakame in warm water for 10 minutes. Drain and squeeze out excess water.

2. Make the Dressing: Whisk together soy sauce, rice vinegar, sesame oil, mirin, ginger, and chili flakes.

3. Combine Ingredients: Toss rehydrated seaweed with the dressing in a large bowl.

4. Serve: Garnish with toasted sesame seeds.

Pro Tip: Add julienned cucumbers for extra crunch and freshness.

Balancing Sweet, Salty, and Spicy Flavors

1. Sweetness
   - Use natural sweeteners like honey, palm sugar, or fruit to soften spicy or salty elements.
   2. Saltiness

- Soy sauce, fish sauce, and miso provide umami and enhance other flavors.
3. Spiciness
- Adjust spice levels with fresh chilies, chili oil, or sriracha.
4. Acidity
- Lime juice or rice vinegar balances sweetness and saltiness for a harmonious dish.

Creative Variations for Asian-Inspired Salads

1. Asian Noodle Salad
Toss soba or rice noodles with vegetables, sesame seeds, and a miso-ginger dressing.
2. Vietnamese Shrimp Salad
Combine grilled shrimp, rice noodles, herbs, and a lime-fish sauce dressing.
3. Korean Spicy Cucumber Salad
Slice cucumbers thinly and toss with gochujang (Korean chili paste), sesame oil, and rice vinegar.

Tips for Making Authentic Asian-Inspired Salads

1. Use Fresh Ingredients
- Prioritize fresh vegetables, herbs, and high-quality oils for the best flavor.
2. Adjust Spice Levels
- Start with mild amounts of chili and adjust to taste.
3. Serve Fresh
- These salads are best served immediately to preserve their crispness and flavor.

Conclusion: Exploring the Bold Flavors of Asia

Asian-inspired salads are a vibrant celebration of flavor, texture, and freshness. With recipes like Thai Green Papaya Salad, Sesame Chicken Salad, and Japanese Seaweed Salad, you can bring the bold and balanced flavors of Asia to your table. Whether you're seeking a light appetizer or a satisfying meal, these salads are versatile, nourishing, and utterly delicious.

In the next chapter, we'll explore the flavors of Latin America, featuring unique ingredients like avocado, corn, and citrus to create salads that are as colorful as they are flavorful. Let's continue our journey through global salads!

Chapter 10: Latin American-Inspired Salads

Latin American-inspired salads are a vibrant fusion of bold spices, fresh ingredients, and dynamic textures. From the smoky flavors of Mexican street corn salad to the creamy richness of avocado and black bean salad, and the refreshing tang of ceviche salad, these dishes capture the essence of Latin American cuisine. Each salad tells a story of its cultural roots, combining ingredients like citrus, chili, herbs, and beans to create memorable and satisfying meals.

This chapter explores three quintessential Latin American salads, shares tips for incorporating bold spices and fresh ingredients, and provides strategies for layering flavors with salsas and dressings. By the end, you'll have the tools and confidence to create authentic and flavorful Latin-inspired salads.

Why Latin American-Inspired Salads?

1. Bursting with Flavor

Latin American salads emphasize bold, balanced flavors, blending smoky, spicy, tangy, and sweet notes.

2. Fresh and Nutritious

These salads feature fresh vegetables, fruits, legumes, and herbs, making them a healthy addition to any meal.

3. Versatile and Satisfying

From light appetizers to hearty mains, Latin American salads can be adapted for any occasion.

Key Ingredients in Latin American Salads

1. Avocado

   - Role: Adds creaminess and richness to salads.

   - How to Use: Dice, slice, or mash into a dressing.

2. Corn

   - Role: Provides sweetness and a tender-crunchy texture.

- How to Use: Grilled, roasted, or fresh off the cob.
3. Black Beans
- Role: Adds heartiness and protein.
- How to Use: Rinse canned beans or cook dried beans until tender.
4. Citrus
- Examples: Lime, lemon, and orange.
- Role: Adds tanginess and brightness to dressings and marinades.
5. Chili Peppers
- Types: Jalapeño, serrano, habanero, or dried chilies.
- Role: Introduces heat and spice, balancing sweet and tangy flavors.
6. Fresh Herbs
- Examples: Cilantro, parsley, oregano.
- Role: Enhances freshness and adds aromatic complexity.

Recipes for Latin American-Inspired Salads

1. Mexican Street Corn Salad (Esquites Salad)

This salad captures the smoky, creamy, and tangy flavors of Mexican street corn, perfect for summer gatherings.

Ingredients (Serves 4):
- 4 cups corn kernels (fresh or frozen, roasted or grilled)
- 1/2 cup cotija cheese, crumbled
- 1/4 cup fresh cilantro, chopped
- 1/4 cup mayonnaise
- 2 tablespoons sour cream
- 1 tablespoon lime juice
- 1 teaspoon chili powder
- 1/2 teaspoon smoked paprika
- Salt and pepper to taste

Instructions:
1. Prepare the Corn: Grill or roast corn until slightly charred. Cool and remove kernels.
2. Make the Dressing: Whisk together mayonnaise, sour cream, lime juice, chili powder, smoked paprika, salt, and pepper.

3. Assemble the Salad: Toss corn with dressing in a large bowl. Mix in cotija cheese and cilantro.

4. Serve: Garnish with extra cheese and cilantro.

Pro Tip: Add diced jalapeño for a spicy kick.

2. Avocado and Black Bean Salad

This hearty salad combines creamy avocado, protein-rich black beans, and vibrant vegetables for a satisfying meal.

Ingredients (Serves 4):

- 2 avocados, diced

- 2 cups cooked black beans

- 1 cup cherry tomatoes, halved

- 1/2 cup red onion, diced

- 1/4 cup fresh cilantro, chopped

- 1/4 cup lime juice

- 2 tablespoons olive oil

- 1 teaspoon cumin

- Salt and pepper to taste

Instructions:

1. Prepare Ingredients: Dice avocado, tomatoes, and onion. Rinse black beans.

2. Make the Dressing: Whisk lime juice, olive oil, cumin, salt, and pepper.

3. Combine Ingredients: Toss avocado, beans, tomatoes, onion, and cilantro with dressing.

4. Serve: Garnish with additional cilantro and serve immediately.

Pro Tip: Add crumbled queso fresco or a handful of corn kernels for added flavor.

3. Ceviche Salad

This refreshing salad uses citrus-marinated seafood, fresh vegetables, and herbs for a light yet flavorful dish.

Ingredients (Serves 4):

- 1 pound white fish or shrimp, diced

- 1/2 cup lime juice

- 1/4 cup lemon juice
- 1/4 cup orange juice
- 1 cup cucumber, diced
- 1/2 cup red onion, finely chopped
- 1/2 cup cherry tomatoes, halved
- 1 jalapeño, finely chopped
- 1/4 cup fresh cilantro, chopped
- Salt and pepper to taste

Instructions:

1. Marinate the Seafood: Combine fish or shrimp with lime, lemon, and orange juice in a bowl. Cover and refrigerate for 20-30 minutes until opaque.

2. Prepare Vegetables: Dice cucumber, onion, and tomatoes.

3. Assemble the Salad: Drain excess citrus juice from seafood. Toss with vegetables, jalapeño, and cilantro.

4. Serve: Season with salt and pepper and serve chilled.

Pro Tip: Add diced mango or avocado for a touch of sweetness.

Incorporating Bold Spices and Fresh Ingredients

1. Use Fresh, High-Quality Ingredients
   - Choose ripe avocados, fresh citrus, and aromatic herbs for maximum flavor.

2. Experiment with Spices
   - Blend spices like cumin, chili powder, smoked paprika, and cayenne to create depth and complexity.

3. Balance Flavors
   - Combine sweet ingredients like mango or corn with tangy citrus and spicy chilies for a harmonious dish.

4. Layer Textures
   - Mix creamy elements (avocado, cheese) with crunchy vegetables (corn, peppers) and tender beans or seafood for variety.

Tips for Layering Flavors with Salsas and Dressings

1. Salsa as a Dressing
   - Use salsas like pico de gallo or tomatillo salsa as a dressing to add freshness and flavor.
   2. Citrus-Based Dressings
   - Combine lime or orange juice with olive oil, honey, and chili flakes for a tangy dressing.
   3. Infused Oils
   - Create chili-infused or garlic-infused oils to drizzle over salads for extra flavor.
   4. Marinated Ingredients
   - Marinate proteins like shrimp or chicken in citrus and spices before adding to the salad.

Creative Variations for Latin American Salads

1. Grilled Shrimp and Mango Salad
   Combine grilled shrimp, diced mango, arugula, and avocado with a chili-lime dressing.
   2. Roasted Sweet Potato and Black Bean Salad
   Toss roasted sweet potatoes with black beans, spinach, and a cumin-lime vinaigrette.
   3. Quinoa and Corn Salad
   Mix cooked quinoa, roasted corn, red peppers, and cilantro with a zesty lime dressing.

Conclusion: Celebrating the Vibrant Flavors of Latin America

Latin American-inspired salads are a celebration of bold flavors, fresh ingredients, and dynamic textures. With recipes like Mexican Street Corn Salad, Avocado and Black Bean Salad, and Ceviche Salad, you can bring the vibrant spirit of Latin America to your table. Whether you're hosting a summer barbecue or looking for a refreshing weeknight dinner, these salads offer endless versatility and satisfaction.

In the next chapter, we'll explore gourmet salads that elevate everyday ingredients into restaurant-quality dishes. Let's continue this culinary adventure!

Chapter 11: European Classics

European salads are steeped in tradition, often serving as cultural icons that reflect the culinary heritage of their origins. From the vibrant and refreshing Niçoise salad of France to the sweet and savory Waldorf salad of America by European influence, and the hearty Russian Olivier salad, these classic recipes showcase the diversity and sophistication of European cuisine.

In this chapter, we'll explore three timeless European salads, delve into the traditions and history behind these dishes, and offer tips on pairing these classics with modern dishes. By understanding the essence of these salads, you'll be able to recreate them authentically and adapt them to suit contemporary tastes.

The Role of Tradition in European Salad-Making

1. Salads as Cultural Artifacts

Classic European salads often have storied origins, reflecting the ingredients, flavors, and culinary practices of their time and place.

- Example: Niçoise salad hails from Nice, France, showcasing the region's reliance on fresh produce, olives, and seafood.

2. Celebration of Ingredients

European salads highlight seasonal and local ingredients, emphasizing quality and freshness over complexity.

3. Balance of Flavors and Textures

Traditional European salads masterfully balance sweet, savory, and tangy elements, with careful attention to texture.

Recipes for European Classic Salads

1. Niçoise Salad

Niçoise salad is a vibrant and versatile dish that reflects the flavors of the Mediterranean. It combines fresh vegetables, tender tuna, and briny olives for a refreshing and satisfying meal.

Ingredients (Serves 4):

- 4 cups mixed greens
- 8 small new potatoes, boiled and halved
- 2 cups green beans, blanched
- 2 cups cherry tomatoes, halved
- 4 hard-boiled eggs, halved
- 1/2 cup Niçoise or Kalamata olives
- 2 cans of tuna in olive oil, drained
- 1/4 cup red onion, thinly sliced
- 1/4 cup olive oil
- 2 tablespoons red wine vinegar
- 1 teaspoon Dijon mustard
- 1 garlic clove, minced
- Salt and pepper to taste

Instructions:

1. Prepare Ingredients: Wash and dry greens. Boil potatoes, blanch green beans, and prepare hard-boiled eggs.

2. Make the Dressing: Whisk together olive oil, red wine vinegar, Dijon mustard, garlic, salt, and pepper.

3. Assemble the Salad: Arrange greens, potatoes, green beans, tomatoes, eggs, olives, and tuna on a large platter.

4. Dress and Serve: Drizzle with dressing and serve immediately.

Pro Tip: Substitute fresh seared tuna for a more upscale presentation.

2. Waldorf Salad

The Waldorf salad originated in New York City's Waldorf Astoria Hotel in the late 19th century but draws heavily on European influences in its combination of apples, celery, and walnuts.

Ingredients (Serves 4):

- 2 cups diced apples (Granny Smith or Gala)
- 1 cup diced celery
- 1/2 cup seedless grapes, halved
- 1/2 cup walnuts, toasted
- 1/4 cup mayonnaise
- 2 tablespoons Greek yogurt (optional)
- 1 tablespoon lemon juice
- Salt and pepper to taste
- 4 cups lettuce leaves for serving

Instructions:

1. Prepare Ingredients: Dice apples and celery, halve grapes, and toast walnuts.

2. Make the Dressing: Whisk together mayonnaise, Greek yogurt, lemon juice, salt, and pepper.

3. Combine Ingredients: Toss apples, celery, grapes, and walnuts with the dressing in a large bowl.

4. Serve: Arrange lettuce leaves on plates and top with the salad.

Pro Tip: Add diced chicken or turkey for a heartier version.

3. Russian Olivier Salad

The Olivier salad, also known as Russian salad, is a creamy and hearty dish traditionally served during celebrations.

Ingredients (Serves 4):

- 3 medium potatoes, boiled and diced
- 2 medium carrots, boiled and diced
- 1 cup green peas, cooked
- 1 cup diced cooked chicken or ham
- 3 hard-boiled eggs, diced
- 1/2 cup pickles, diced
- 1/4 cup red onion, finely chopped
- 1/2 cup mayonnaise
- 1 tablespoon Dijon mustard
- Salt and pepper to taste

Instructions:

1. Prepare Ingredients: Boil and dice potatoes, carrots, and eggs. Cook peas if using fresh or frozen.

2. Combine Ingredients: In a large bowl, mix potatoes, carrots, peas, chicken or ham, eggs, pickles, and onion.

3. Make the Dressing: Whisk together mayonnaise, Dijon mustard, salt, and pepper.

4. Toss and Serve: Mix dressing with salad and refrigerate for at least 30 minutes before serving.

Pro Tip: Garnish with fresh dill or parsley for added flavor.

Pairing Classic European Salads with Modern Dishes

1. Niçoise Salad
    - Pairing Ideas:
    - Grilled fish or seafood, such as salmon or shrimp.
    - A crisp white wine like Sauvignon Blanc or a dry rosé.
2. Waldorf Salad
    - Pairing Ideas:
    - Roasted turkey or chicken breast for a holiday-inspired meal.
    - A light, fruity Chardonnay.
3. Russian Olivier Salad
    - Pairing Ideas:
    - Served alongside grilled sausages or roasted pork.
    - A glass of chilled vodka or sparkling water with lemon.

Modern Twists on European Classics

1. Mediterranean Waldorf Salad
    - Swap mayonnaise for a lemon-tahini dressing and add fresh parsley and feta cheese.
    2. Deconstructed Niçoise Salad
    - Arrange ingredients on individual plates for a modern, elegant presentation.

3. Vegan Olivier Salad

- Replace mayonnaise with a cashew-based dressing and use chickpeas instead of chicken or ham.

Tips for Mastering European Classic Salads

1. Use High-Quality Ingredients

- Fresh, seasonal produce and authentic ingredients like Niçoise olives or cotija cheese ensure the best results.

2. Focus on Presentation

- Classic European salads often emphasize aesthetics. Arrange ingredients neatly for visual appeal.

3. Adapt to Modern Tastes

- Use lighter dressings, incorporate whole grains, or add plant-based proteins to cater to contemporary preferences.

Conclusion: Embracing the Elegance of European Salads

European classic salads like Niçoise, Waldorf, and Olivier celebrate the rich culinary traditions of their regions. By mastering these recipes and pairing them with modern dishes, you can bring a touch of timeless elegance to your meals. Whether you're hosting a formal dinner or enjoying a casual lunch, these salads offer a perfect blend of history, flavor, and sophistication.

In the next chapter, we'll explore gourmet salads that elevate everyday ingredients into restaurant-quality dishes, showcasing the artistry and creativity of modern salad-making. Let's continue crafting exceptional salads!

Chapter 12: Spring Salads

Spring is a season of renewal and abundance, offering a vibrant array of fresh, tender produce that breathes new life into our kitchens. As the frost melts and the first crops of the year arrive, spring salads become a celebration of crisp textures, bright flavors, and colorful presentations. With ingredients like asparagus, peas, radishes, arugula, and strawberries, spring salads are light, refreshing, and packed with nutrients.

In this chapter, we'll explore three quintessential spring salads: Asparagus and Pea Salad, Radish and Arugula Salad, and Strawberry Spinach Salad. You'll learn how to make the most of spring's bounty, craft light and refreshing dressings, and embrace the essence of the season in every bite.

The Appeal of Spring Salads

1. A Celebration of Freshness

Spring salads are defined by their reliance on fresh, seasonal ingredients. Crisp vegetables, sweet fruits, and tender greens come together to create dishes that are as beautiful as they are delicious.

2. Light and Nutritious

Spring salads are naturally light, making them ideal for healthy meals and detox-friendly diets. They're often paired with simple, flavorful dressings that enhance, rather than overpower, the natural flavors of the ingredients.

3. Versatile and Vibrant

From casual lunches to elegant dinner parties, spring salads are versatile enough to suit any occasion. Their vibrant colors and textures make them visually stunning and satisfying.

Key Ingredients in Spring Salads

1. Asparagus
   - Flavor: Mild and earthy, with a slightly sweet undertone.
   - Best Use: Blanched or grilled for salads.

2. Peas
- Flavor: Sweet and tender.
- Best Use: Fresh or lightly steamed for texture and flavor.
3. Radishes
- Flavor: Peppery and crisp.
- Best Use: Thinly sliced or shaved for a vibrant crunch.
4. Arugula
- Flavor: Peppery and slightly bitter.
- Best Use: A bold base for spring salads.
5. Strawberries
- Flavor: Sweet and tangy.
- Best Use: Freshly sliced, adding a burst of sweetness.

Recipes for Spring Salads

1. Asparagus and Pea Salad

This vibrant salad highlights the sweetness of peas and the earthy flavor of asparagus, complemented by a zesty lemon dressing.

Ingredients (Serves 4):
- 1 bunch asparagus, trimmed and blanched
- 1 cup fresh peas, blanched
- 1/4 cup shaved Parmesan cheese
- 1/4 cup toasted almonds, sliced
- 4 cups mixed spring greens (baby spinach, arugula, or butter lettuce)
- 1/4 cup olive oil
- 2 tablespoons lemon juice
- 1 teaspoon Dijon mustard
- Salt and pepper to taste

Instructions:

1. Prepare Vegetables: Blanch asparagus and peas in boiling water for 2-3 minutes, then transfer to an ice bath to cool.

2. Make the Dressing: Whisk together olive oil, lemon juice, Dijon mustard, salt, and pepper.

3. Assemble the Salad: Arrange greens, asparagus, peas, Parmesan, and almonds in a large bowl.

4. Dress and Serve: Drizzle with dressing and toss gently.

Pro Tip: Add a soft-boiled egg for extra protein and richness.

2. Radish and Arugula Salad

This crisp, peppery salad is balanced with a tangy vinaigrette and crunchy toppings for a refreshing bite.

Ingredients (Serves 4):

- 4 cups arugula

- 1 cup radishes, thinly sliced

- 1/4 cup red onion, thinly sliced

- 1/4 cup crumbled goat cheese

- 1/4 cup sunflower seeds

- 1/4 cup olive oil

- 2 tablespoons apple cider vinegar

- 1 teaspoon honey

- Salt and pepper to taste

Instructions:

1. Prepare Vegetables: Wash and dry arugula. Thinly slice radishes and onions.

2. Make the Dressing: Whisk together olive oil, apple cider vinegar, honey, salt, and pepper.

3. Assemble the Salad: Combine arugula, radishes, onion, goat cheese, and sunflower seeds in a large bowl.

4. Dress and Serve: Toss with dressing and serve immediately.

Pro Tip: Add a handful of microgreens for an extra layer of texture and flavor.

3. Strawberry Spinach Salad

This sweet and tangy salad pairs fresh strawberries with tender spinach and a balsamic poppy seed dressing.

Ingredients (Serves 4):

- 4 cups baby spinach

- 1 cup fresh strawberries, sliced
- 1/4 cup feta cheese, crumbled
- 1/4 cup candied pecans
- 1/4 cup red onion, thinly sliced
- 1/4 cup olive oil
- 2 tablespoons balsamic vinegar
- 1 teaspoon honey
- 1 teaspoon poppy seeds
- Salt and pepper to taste

Instructions:

1. Prepare Ingredients: Wash and dry spinach. Slice strawberries and onions.

2. Make the Dressing: Whisk together olive oil, balsamic vinegar, honey, poppy seeds, salt, and pepper.

3. Assemble the Salad: Combine spinach, strawberries, feta, pecans, and onion in a large bowl.

4. Dress and Serve: Drizzle with dressing and toss gently.

Pro Tip: Add grilled chicken or shrimp for a heartier meal.

Light and Refreshing Dressings for Spring Salads

1. Lemon Herb Dressing

A bright, zesty dressing that pairs beautifully with asparagus and peas.

Ingredients:

- 1/4 cup olive oil
- 2 tablespoons lemon juice
- 1 teaspoon Dijon mustard
- 1 tablespoon fresh dill, chopped
- Salt and pepper to taste

2. Honey Cider Vinaigrette

A sweet and tangy dressing ideal for arugula and radish salads.

Ingredients:

- 1/4 cup apple cider vinegar

- 1/4 cup olive oil
- 1 teaspoon honey
- 1/2 teaspoon Dijon mustard
- Salt and pepper to taste

3. Balsamic Poppy Seed Dressing

A sweet and savory option for strawberry spinach salad.

Ingredients:
- 1/4 cup balsamic vinegar
- 1/4 cup olive oil
- 1 teaspoon honey
- 1 teaspoon poppy seeds
- Salt and pepper to taste

Tips for Using Fresh, Tender Spring Produce

1. Shop Seasonally
- Visit farmers' markets for the freshest spring produce.
2. Handle Ingredients Gently
- Use light dressings to avoid overwhelming delicate greens and vegetables.
3. Embrace Simplicity
- Let the natural flavors of spring ingredients shine by keeping preparations simple.

Pairing Spring Salads with Main Dishes

1. Asparagus and Pea Salad
- Serve with grilled salmon or roasted chicken for a complete meal.
2. Radish and Arugula Salad
- Pair with a crusty baguette and soft cheese for a light lunch.
3. Strawberry Spinach Salad
- Complement with grilled shrimp or a glass of rosé wine.

Conclusion: Welcoming Spring with Fresh Flavors

Spring salads are a joyful celebration of the season's best ingredients. By incorporating fresh, tender produce like asparagus, peas, radishes, and strawberries, and pairing them with light, flavorful dressings, you can create dishes that are as beautiful as they are delicious. Whether you're preparing an elegant dinner or a casual picnic, these salads bring the spirit of spring to your table.

In the next chapter, we'll explore the bounty of summer salads, focusing on juicy tomatoes, crisp cucumbers, and vibrant herbs to create refreshing dishes for the warmer months. Let's continue savoring the seasons!

Chapter 13: Summer Salads

Summer salads are the ultimate celebration of the season's vibrant produce, from juicy tomatoes and crisp cucumbers to sweet watermelon and freshly grilled corn. These salads are light, refreshing, and bursting with flavor, making them the perfect addition to barbecues, picnics, or sunny alfresco dining. They are also versatile, pairing well with grilled proteins or standing alone as star dishes.

In this chapter, we'll explore three quintessential summer salads: Caprese Salad, Watermelon and Feta Salad, and Grilled Corn Salad. You'll learn how to make the most of summer's bounty, incorporate fresh herbs and grilled ingredients, and keep your salads cool and crisp in the heat.

The Beauty of Summer Salads

1. A Celebration of Seasonal Produce

Summer salads showcase the best of the season's fruits, vegetables, and herbs, highlighting their natural sweetness and freshness.

2. Light and Refreshing

With high water content and minimal cooking, summer salads provide hydration and cooling relief during hot days.

3. Versatile and Crowd-Pleasing

From casual family gatherings to elegant dinner parties, summer salads can be easily adapted to suit any occasion.

Key Ingredients in Summer Salads

1. Tomatoes

- Flavor: Sweet, tangy, and slightly acidic.
- Best Use: Use heirloom or vine-ripened tomatoes for maximum flavor in salads.

2. Watermelon

- Flavor: Sweet and juicy, with a crisp texture.

- Best Use: Pairs well with salty cheeses and fresh herbs.
3. Corn
- Flavor: Sweet and slightly nutty.
- Best Use: Grilled or roasted for added smokiness.
4. Fresh Herbs
- Examples: Basil, mint, cilantro, and dill.
- Best Use: Add brightness and aromatic depth to salads.
5. Soft Cheeses
- Examples: Mozzarella, feta, or goat cheese.
- Best Use: Provide creaminess and contrast to crisp fruits and vegetables.

Recipes for Summer Salads

1. Caprese Salad

The Caprese Salad is a classic Italian dish that celebrates the perfect trio of ripe tomatoes, creamy mozzarella, and fresh basil.

Ingredients (Serves 4):
- 4 large ripe tomatoes, sliced
- 8 ounces fresh mozzarella, sliced
- 1/4 cup fresh basil leaves
- 2 tablespoons extra-virgin olive oil
- 1 tablespoon balsamic glaze
- Salt and pepper to taste

Instructions:

1. Slice Ingredients: Slice tomatoes and mozzarella into even rounds.

2. Assemble the Salad: Arrange tomato and mozzarella slices on a platter, alternating them in a circular pattern.

3. Add Basil: Tuck basil leaves between the layers.

4. Dress and Serve: Drizzle with olive oil and balsamic glaze. Sprinkle with salt and pepper to taste.

Pro Tip: Use heirloom tomatoes for a colorful and flavorful presentation.

2. Watermelon and Feta Salad

This salad combines the sweetness of watermelon with the saltiness of feta, accented by fresh mint for a refreshing summer dish.

Ingredients (Serves 4):

- 4 cups cubed watermelon

- 1/2 cup crumbled feta cheese

- 1/4 cup fresh mint leaves, chopped

- 2 tablespoons lime juice

- 1 tablespoon olive oil

- Salt and pepper to taste

Instructions:

1. Prepare Ingredients: Cube watermelon and chop mint.

2. Assemble the Salad: Combine watermelon, feta, and mint in a large bowl.

3. Dress and Serve: Drizzle with lime juice and olive oil. Toss gently and season with salt and pepper.

Pro Tip: Add sliced cucumbers or a handful of arugula for extra texture and flavor.

3. Grilled Corn Salad

Grilled corn brings a smoky sweetness to this vibrant summer salad, enhanced by fresh herbs and a tangy lime dressing.

Ingredients (Serves 4):

- 4 ears of corn, husked

- 1 cup cherry tomatoes, halved

- 1/4 cup red onion, diced

- 1/4 cup fresh cilantro, chopped

- 2 tablespoons lime juice

- 2 tablespoons olive oil

- 1/2 teaspoon chili powder

- Salt and pepper to taste

Instructions:

1. Grill the Corn: Preheat grill to medium-high. Grill corn for 8-10 minutes, turning occasionally, until charred. Let cool and cut kernels off the cob.

2. Prepare Vegetables: Halve cherry tomatoes and dice red onion.

3. Assemble the Salad: Combine corn, tomatoes, onion, and cilantro in a large bowl.

4. Make the Dressing: Whisk lime juice, olive oil, chili powder, salt, and pepper.

5. Dress and Serve: Toss salad with dressing and serve immediately.

Pro Tip: Add crumbled cotija cheese or diced avocado for a heartier version.

Highlighting Summer Fruits, Herbs, and Grilled Ingredients

1. Summer Fruits
   - Use fruits like peaches, berries, and melons for a natural sweetness.
   - Pair with salty or tangy ingredients, such as feta or balsamic vinegar, for contrast.

2. Fresh Herbs
   - Use herbs like basil, mint, and dill liberally to add freshness and complexity.

3. Grilled Ingredients
   - Grilling enhances the natural sweetness of vegetables like corn, zucchini, and bell peppers.
   - Brush with olive oil and season with salt before grilling for added flavor.

Tips for Keeping Salads Cool and Crisp in the Heat

1. Chill Ingredients
   - Refrigerate greens, fruits, and vegetables before assembling your salad.
2. Use Ice Baths

- After blanching vegetables like beans or peas, transfer them to an ice bath to preserve their crispness.

3. Serve on Chilled Plates

- Use chilled bowls or plates to keep salads fresh during serving.

4. Add Dressing Just Before Serving

- Prevent wilting by dressing salads immediately before serving.

Creative Variations for Summer Salads

1. Peach and Burrata Salad

Combine sliced peaches, creamy burrata, arugula, and a drizzle of honey-balsamic dressing.

2. Grilled Vegetable and Quinoa Salad

Toss grilled zucchini, bell peppers, and red onions with cooked quinoa and a lemon-herb dressing.

3. Berry Spinach Salad

Mix fresh spinach, strawberries, blueberries, goat cheese, and candied pecans with a poppy seed dressing.

Pairing Summer Salads with Main Dishes

1. Caprese Salad

- Pair with grilled chicken or fresh focaccia for a simple Italian-inspired meal.

2. Watermelon and Feta Salad

- Serve alongside grilled fish or lamb for a light, refreshing complement.

3. Grilled Corn Salad

- Perfect with barbecued ribs, pulled pork, or veggie burgers.

Conclusion: Embracing the Flavors of Summer

Summer salads are a celebration of the season's freshest ingredients, combining fruits, herbs, and grilled elements to create dishes that are light, vibrant, and satisfying. Whether it's the classic elegance of Caprese Salad, the refreshing sweetness of Watermelon and Feta Salad, or the smoky richness of Grilled Corn Salad, these recipes capture the essence of summer.

In the next chapter, we'll transition into the warm, earthy flavors of fall salads, featuring hearty ingredients like squash, apples, and nuts. Let's continue savoring the seasons!

Chapter 14: Autumn and Winter Salads

As the air turns crisp and the days grow shorter, the produce of autumn and winter brings a bounty of earthy, hearty flavors to our kitchens. While salads are often associated with summer, they can also be comforting, nourishing meals during colder months. By incorporating roasted vegetables, whole grains, and warm dressings, you can create salads that are as satisfying as any hot dish.

This chapter delves into three classic autumn and winter salads: Roasted Beet Salad, Brussels Sprout Slaw, and Warm Farro Salad. You'll learn how to make the most of seasonal ingredients, create hearty textures, and craft warm dressings that bring a sense of comfort to every bite.

Why Autumn and Winter Salads?

1. Seasonal Ingredients
   The cooler months bring a wealth of hearty produce like root vegetables, winter squash, Brussels sprouts, and dark leafy greens. These ingredients are perfect for robust salads.
   2. Comforting Textures
   Roasted vegetables, toasted nuts, and whole grains add a depth of flavor and texture that feels cozy and satisfying.
   3. Versatile and Nutritious
   These salads are nutrient-dense and versatile enough to serve as side dishes or mains, making them ideal for holiday gatherings or everyday meals.

Key Ingredients in Autumn and Winter Salads

1. Root Vegetables
   - Examples: Beets, carrots, parsnips, and sweet potatoes.
   - Best Use: Roasted or steamed to enhance their natural sweetness.

2. Hearty Greens
- Examples: Kale, spinach, arugula, and mustard greens.
- Best Use: Massaged raw for tenderness or lightly wilted for warmth.
3. Brussels Sprouts
- Flavor: Nutty and slightly bitter.
- Best Use: Thinly shaved for slaws or roasted for salads.
4. Whole Grains
- Examples: Farro, barley, quinoa, and wild rice.
- Best Use: Cooked to al dente and mixed with vegetables for hearty textures.
5. Warm Dressings
- Examples: Maple vinaigrette, mustard-based dressings, and balsamic reductions.
- Best Use: Add depth and warmth to complement earthy ingredients.

Recipes for Autumn and Winter Salads

1. Roasted Beet Salad

This vibrant salad combines the earthiness of roasted beets with the creaminess of goat cheese and the crunch of toasted walnuts.
Ingredients (Serves 4):
- 4 medium beets, roasted and sliced
- 4 cups arugula or mixed greens
- 1/4 cup crumbled goat cheese
- 1/4 cup walnuts, toasted
- 2 tablespoons balsamic vinegar
- 2 tablespoons olive oil
- 1 teaspoon Dijon mustard
- Salt and pepper to taste
Instructions:
1. Roast the Beets: Preheat oven to 400°F (200°C). Wrap beets in foil and roast for 45-60 minutes until tender. Peel and slice when cool.
2. Make the Dressing: Whisk together balsamic vinegar, olive oil, Dijon mustard, salt, and pepper.

3. Assemble the Salad: Arrange greens, beets, goat cheese, and walnuts on a platter.

4. Dress and Serve: Drizzle with dressing and toss gently.

Pro Tip: Add orange segments for a citrusy twist.

2. Brussels Sprout Slaw

This crisp slaw combines shaved Brussels sprouts with a tangy apple cider dressing and crunchy almonds.

Ingredients (Serves 4):

- 4 cups Brussels sprouts, thinly shaved
- 1 apple, julienned
- 1/4 cup almonds, sliced and toasted
- 1/4 cup dried cranberries
- 2 tablespoons apple cider vinegar
- 2 tablespoons olive oil
- 1 teaspoon honey
- 1/2 teaspoon Dijon mustard
- Salt and pepper to taste

Instructions:

1. Shave the Brussels Sprouts: Use a mandoline or sharp knife to slice Brussels sprouts thinly.

2. Make the Dressing: Whisk together apple cider vinegar, olive oil, honey, Dijon mustard, salt, and pepper.

3. Combine Ingredients: Toss Brussels sprouts, apple, almonds, and cranberries in a large bowl.

4. Dress and Serve: Drizzle with dressing and mix well.

Pro Tip: Add shredded Parmesan for an extra layer of flavor.

3. Warm Farro Salad

This hearty grain salad features nutty farro, roasted squash, and a warm maple dressing for a comforting winter dish.

Ingredients (Serves 4):

- 1 cup farro, cooked
- 2 cups butternut squash, diced and roasted
- 1/4 cup pumpkin seeds, toasted
- 1/4 cup dried cherries or raisins
- 2 cups baby kale or spinach
- 3 tablespoons olive oil
- 2 tablespoons maple syrup
- 1 tablespoon apple cider vinegar
- 1 teaspoon Dijon mustard
- Salt and pepper to taste

Instructions:

1. Cook Farro: Rinse and cook farro according to package instructions. Drain and set aside.

2. Roast the Squash: Toss diced squash with olive oil, salt, and pepper. Roast at 400°F (200°C) for 25-30 minutes until tender.

3. Make the Dressing: In a small saucepan, heat olive oil, maple syrup, apple cider vinegar, and Dijon mustard until warm. Season with salt and pepper.

4. Assemble the Salad: Combine farro, squash, pumpkin seeds, dried cherries, and greens in a large bowl.

5. Dress and Serve: Pour warm dressing over the salad and toss gently.

Pro Tip: Add crumbled goat cheese or feta for extra creaminess.

How to Make Salads Comforting During Colder Months

1. Use Warm Ingredients

Incorporate roasted vegetables, cooked grains, or proteins to make salads hearty and satisfying.

2. Add Crunch and Creaminess

Balance textures with toasted nuts, seeds, and creamy cheeses like goat cheese or feta.

3. Include Sweet and Savory Elements

Blend sweet ingredients (dried fruits, maple syrup) with savory flavors (roasted vegetables, nuts) for depth.

4. Embrace Earthy Flavors

Choose ingredients like beets, Brussels sprouts, and squash for their rich, earthy profiles.

Tips for Working with Hearty Vegetables and Grains

1. Roast Vegetables for Sweetness

Roasting enhances the natural sugars in vegetables, making them sweeter and more flavorful.

2. Cook Grains to Al Dente

Ensure grains like farro and barley are cooked but retain some chewiness for texture.

3. Massage Tough Greens

Rub kale or mustard greens with a pinch of salt and olive oil to soften their texture and reduce bitterness.

4. Toast Nuts and Seeds

Toasting nuts and seeds enhances their flavor and adds a satisfying crunch.

Pairing Autumn and Winter Salads with Main Dishes

1. Roasted Beet Salad
   - Serve with grilled salmon or a roasted pork tenderloin.
2. Brussels Sprout Slaw
   - Pair with roasted chicken or a hearty vegetarian stew.
3. Warm Farro Salad
   - Complement with braised short ribs or a creamy squash soup.

Creative Variations for Autumn and Winter Salads

1. Pear and Blue Cheese Salad

Combine roasted pears, blue cheese, walnuts, and arugula with a balsamic dressing.

2. Wild Rice and Cranberry Salad

Mix wild rice, dried cranberries, toasted pecans, and kale with a honey-mustard vinaigrette.

3. Sweet Potato and Chickpea Salad

Roast sweet potatoes and chickpeas, then toss with spinach and a tahini-lemon dressing.

Conclusion: Embracing Comfort in Cold Weather

Autumn and winter salads bring warmth, heartiness, and comfort to the table with seasonal ingredients, earthy flavors, and creative textures. Whether it's the vibrant Roasted Beet Salad, the crisp and tangy Brussels Sprout Slaw, or the comforting Warm Farro Salad, these dishes showcase the versatility and richness of cold-weather produce.

In the next chapter, we'll conclude our journey with tips and inspiration for creating your own signature salads, blending global flavors, seasonal ingredients, and personal creativity to craft dishes that truly stand out. Let's continue celebrating the art of salad-making!

Chapter 15: Creative and Show-Stopping Salads

Salads can be more than just a side dish; they can be the star of any meal, showcasing creativity, flavor, and visual appeal. A show-stopping salad combines delicious ingredients with a flair for presentation, transforming a simple dish into a work of art. Whether it's an intricately layered Mason jar salad, a towering fruit and nut creation, or a vibrant edible flower salad, these dishes leave a lasting impression on your guests.

In this chapter, we'll explore how to craft three innovative and eye-catching salads, share tips for presentation and garnishing, and provide inspiration for elevating your salad-making skills. By the end, you'll have the tools to create salads that not only taste amazing but also look stunning on any table.

The Art of Presentation in Salads

1. Visual Appeal

A beautifully presented salad can set the tone for an entire meal, creating excitement and anticipation.

2. Layering Flavors

By carefully arranging ingredients, you can highlight the colors, textures, and flavors of your salad, ensuring every bite is balanced.

3. Creativity in Design

Using unique plating techniques or unexpected ingredients like edible flowers or layered jars can elevate your salad to the realm of fine dining.

Key Elements of Show-Stopping Salads

1. Vibrant Colors

- Use a mix of colorful vegetables, fruits, and garnishes to make your salad visually striking.

2. Unique Textures

- Combine crunchy, creamy, chewy, and crisp elements for an engaging eating experience.

3. Artful Plating

- Arrange ingredients with intention, using symmetry, layering, or height to create a visual masterpiece.

Recipes for Creative and Show-Stopping Salads

1. Fruit and Nut Salad Towers

This elegant salad features layers of fresh fruits, nuts, and greens, stacked into a visually stunning tower.

Ingredients (Serves 4):

- 4 cups mixed greens (arugula, spinach, or kale)

- 1 cup sliced strawberries

- 1 cup diced pears

- 1/2 cup candied pecans

- 1/4 cup crumbled blue cheese

- 1/4 cup pomegranate seeds

- 1/4 cup balsamic glaze

- 1 tablespoon honey

Instructions:

1. Prepare Ingredients: Wash greens and slice fruits.

2. Build the Towers: Use a metal ring mold to layer greens, strawberries, pears, and pecans on individual plates.

3. Garnish: Top each tower with blue cheese and pomegranate seeds.

4. Dress and Serve: Drizzle with balsamic glaze and honey. Carefully remove the mold before serving.

Pro Tip: Use thinly sliced beets or apples as base layers for added stability and color contrast.

2. Layered Mason Jar Salads

These portable salads are perfect for picnics, lunch prep, or casual gatherings, with each layer showcasing vibrant ingredients.

Ingredients (Serves 4):

- 1 cup cooked quinoa

- 1 cup cherry tomatoes, halved

- 1 cup cucumbers, diced
- 1 cup shredded carrots
- 1/2 cup chickpeas, rinsed and drained
- 4 cups mixed greens
- 1/4 cup olive oil
- 2 tablespoons lemon juice
- 1 teaspoon Dijon mustard
- Salt and pepper to taste

Instructions:

1. Prepare Ingredients: Cook quinoa and chop vegetables.

2. Make the Dressing: Whisk olive oil, lemon juice, Dijon mustard, salt, and pepper. Pour dressing into the bottom of each Mason jar.

3. Layer Ingredients: Add quinoa, chickpeas, carrots, cucumbers, tomatoes, and greens in that order.

4. Seal and Serve: Screw on lids and refrigerate. Shake to mix before eating.

Pro Tip: Add protein like grilled chicken or tofu for a complete meal.

3. Edible Flower Salad

This whimsical salad uses edible flowers to create a vibrant, garden-inspired dish that is as beautiful as it is delicious.

Ingredients (Serves 4):
- 4 cups mixed baby greens
- 1/2 cup thinly sliced radishes
- 1/4 cup shredded carrots
- 1/4 cup edible flowers (pansies, nasturtiums, or violets)
- 1/4 cup goat cheese, crumbled
- 1/4 cup toasted sunflower seeds
- 2 tablespoons raspberry vinaigrette

Instructions:

1. Prepare Ingredients: Wash greens, slice radishes, and shred carrots.

2. Arrange the Salad: Gently toss greens, radishes, and carrots. Place on a platter or individual plates.

3. Add Garnishes: Sprinkle with goat cheese, sunflower seeds, and edible flowers.

4. Dress and Serve: Drizzle with raspberry vinaigrette and serve immediately.

Pro Tip: Always source edible flowers from reputable growers to ensure they are safe for consumption.

Tips for Presentation and Garnishing

1. Use Height and Layers
   - Stack ingredients or use ring molds to create visually dynamic salads.
   2. Highlight Star Ingredients
   - Arrange key ingredients on top or in visible layers to draw attention.
   3. Play with Color Contrast
   - Pair vibrant greens with bright fruits, colorful vegetables, and contrasting garnishes.
   4. Add Finishing Touches
   - Use microgreens, toasted nuts, edible flowers, or herb sprigs as garnishes for an elegant finish.

How to Impress Guests with Innovative Salad Ideas

1. Personalize Your Presentation
   - Serve individual portions using small plates, Mason jars, or glass bowls.
   2. Incorporate Unexpected Ingredients
   - Surprise guests with unique additions like edible flowers, fruit powders, or flavored oils.
   3. Match the Theme
   - Tailor your salad to the event, such as a patriotic color scheme for Independence Day or autumnal flavors for Thanksgiving.
   4. Use Unconventional Platters
   - Present salads on slate boards, wooden trays, or in hollowed-out fruits or vegetables for a creative twist.

Creative Variations for Show-Stopping Salads

1. Tropical Fruit Salad Tower

Layer pineapple, mango, papaya, and arugula, topped with coconut flakes and a lime-honey dressing.

2. Mediterranean Mason Jar Salad

Combine couscous, roasted vegetables, feta cheese, and olives, dressed with lemon-oregano vinaigrette.

3. Floral Caprese Salad

Alternate slices of heirloom tomatoes and mozzarella with basil leaves and edible flowers, drizzled with balsamic reduction.

Conclusion: Elevating Salads to Art

Creative and show-stopping salads allow you to express your culinary artistry while delighting your guests with unexpected flavors and presentations. Whether it's the elegance of Fruit and Nut Salad Towers, the convenience of Layered Mason Jar Salads, or the whimsy of Edible Flower Salads, these dishes prove that salads can be much more than just a healthy option—they can be the centerpiece of any table.

As you continue your salad-making journey, let your imagination run wild and embrace the endless possibilities of this versatile dish. The art of salad-making is not just about nourishment but about creativity, joy, and connection. Now, it's your turn to innovate, impress, and inspire with your own signature creations.

Conclusion: The Endless Potential of Salads

Salads have transcended their role as simple side dishes to become stars of the culinary world, offering infinite possibilities for creativity, flavor, and nourishment. From light and refreshing summer salads to hearty autumn creations, from traditional recipes to show-stopping innovations, salads have the versatility to suit every season, palate, and occasion. They can be quick and simple or elaborate and artistic, showcasing your culinary skills and the beauty of fresh ingredients.

In this final chapter, we'll recap the versatility of salads, encourage you to experiment with ingredients and techniques, and reflect on the joys of making salads a central part of your cooking repertoire. Whether you're a seasoned chef or a home cook looking to expand your skills, salads offer endless opportunities for exploration and delight.

The Versatility of Salads

1. A Dish for Every Season

Salads are a celebration of nature's bounty, adapting effortlessly to the seasons:

- Spring: Fresh greens, peas, and asparagus for light, rejuvenating dishes.
- Summer: Juicy tomatoes, cucumbers, and stone fruits for vibrant and cooling meals.
- Autumn: Roasted root vegetables, grains, and warm dressings for comfort and warmth.
- Winter: Hearty greens, citrus fruits, and nuts to brighten the cold months.

2. Adaptable to Every Meal

Salads can complement any meal or stand alone as the centerpiece:

- Appetizers: Small, artful salads set the tone for a meal.

- Sides: Enhance the main dish with a salad that complements its flavors.

- Main Courses: Add protein, grains, and hearty ingredients for a complete meal.

- Desserts: Fruit-based salads offer a refreshing end to a meal.

3. Endless Combinations of Ingredients

The combinations of greens, vegetables, fruits, proteins, grains, nuts, seeds, and dressings are truly infinite. Each ingredient brings its own flavor, texture, and character, allowing for limitless experimentation.

Encouragement to Experiment

1. Explore Global Flavors

Draw inspiration from cuisines around the world to expand your salad repertoire:

- Asian: Sesame oil, ginger, and soy-based dressings.

- Mediterranean: Olives, feta, and fresh herbs.

- Latin American: Avocado, lime, and chili.

- European: Creamy dressings, nuts, and root vegetables.

2. Play with Textures

A great salad balances crunch, creaminess, tenderness, and chewiness. Experiment with:

- Crunchy: Nuts, seeds, croutons, or crispy vegetables.

- Creamy: Avocado, soft cheeses, or dressings.

- Chewy: Dried fruits, roasted grains, or cooked legumes.

3. Get Creative with Presentation

The way a salad is presented can transform it into a show-stopping dish. Consider:

- Layering: Create visually appealing Mason jar salads.

- Garnishing: Use edible flowers, herbs, or microgreens for a finishing touch.

- Plating: Arrange ingredients artfully on a platter for an elegant presentation.

4. Experiment with Dressings

A dressing can make or break a salad, so don't be afraid to try new combinations:

- Blend oils, vinegars, citrus juices, herbs, and spices to craft your own unique flavors.

- Add unexpected ingredients like tahini, yogurt, or miso for richness.

Salads as a Central Part of Your Culinary Repertoire

1. Health and Nutrition

Salads are inherently nutritious, packed with vitamins, minerals, and antioxidants. By incorporating fresh, whole ingredients, salads can become a cornerstone of a balanced diet.

2. Sustainability

Using seasonal and local ingredients in your salads reduces waste, supports local farmers, and aligns with sustainable cooking practices.

3. Creativity and Self-Expression

Salads offer a platform for culinary creativity, allowing you to experiment, innovate, and express your personal style.

4. Accessibility and Convenience

Salads can be as simple or complex as you like, making them accessible to cooks of all skill levels. With minimal equipment and preparation, anyone can create a delicious salad.

Final Thoughts on Salads

Salads are more than just a collection of ingredients; they are an opportunity to celebrate food in its most natural, vibrant form. Whether you're crafting a quick weekday lunch, preparing an elaborate dish for a special occasion, or exploring the flavors of a new cuisine, salads invite you to engage with your ingredients, your creativity, and your love for cooking.

Actionable Takeaways

1. Keep Experimenting
- Use the recipes and techniques in this book as a foundation, and don't hesitate to experiment with new ingredients, combinations, and presentations.
2. Focus on Freshness
- Prioritize fresh, seasonal ingredients for the best flavors and textures.
3. Invest in Quality Dressings
- A well-crafted dressing elevates even the simplest salad, so take time to perfect your favorite recipes or explore new ones.
4. Make Salads a Habit
- Incorporate salads into your regular meals, using them as a platform for creativity, health, and enjoyment.

A Final Word

Salads are a testament to the beauty of simplicity and the power of creativity. They remind us that even the most humble ingredients can be transformed into something extraordinary with a little care, attention, and imagination. As you continue your culinary journey, let salads inspire you to explore, innovate, and share the joy of good food with others.

Thank you for embarking on this journey through the art of salad-making. May your salads always be fresh, flavorful, and full of life. Here's to endless possibilities and countless delicious creations—happy cooking!

Don't miss out!

Visit the website below and you can sign up to receive emails whenever Olivia Bennett publishes a new book. There's no charge and no obligation.

https://books2read.com/r/B-A-QLEKD-LLIAG

BOOKS2READ

Connecting independent readers to independent writers.

About the Author

Olivia Bennett is a celebrated food writer and chef with expertise spanning multiple culinary disciplines. With a passion for making home cooking accessible, she specializes in guiding readers through everything from hearty casseroles to delicate pastries. Her work is known for its clear instructions, practical tips, and deep understanding of both traditional and modern cooking techniques.

www.ingramcontent.com/pod-product-compliance
Lightning Source LLC
Chambersburg PA
CBHW031431130726
47989CB00003B/1085